S0-BSB-210

# THE CHURCH AND THE JEWISH PEOPLE

# THE CHURCH AND THE JEWISH PEOPLE

Contributions *by*

STEPHEN NEILL

K. H. RENGSTORF

GÖSTA LINDESKOG

H. J. SCHOEPS

R. C. MACANNA

HANS KOSMALA

LEO BAECK

W. W. SIMPSON

H. L. ELLISON

GÖTE HEDENQUIST

W. A. CURTIS

ROBERT SMITH

*Edited by*

GÖTE HEDENQUIST

*Director of The International Missionary Council's
Committee on the Christian Approach to the Jews*

EDINBURGH HOUSE PRESS
2 EATON GATE, LONDON, S.W.1

*1954*

*First Published 1954*

32090

Jan. 1955

MADE AND PRINTED IN GREAT BRITAIN BY
MORRISON AND GIBB LIMITED, LONDON AND EDINBURGH

# PREFACE

AT the World Council of Churches Assembly in Amsterdam, 1948, it was resolved that 'the Assembly recognizes the need for more detailed study by the World Council of Churches of the many complex problems which exist in the field of relations between Christians and Jews'. In order to follow up this resolution, in March 1949, the Right Rev. Bishop Stephen Neill, who at that time was Associate General Secretary of the W.C.C., called a Committee Meeting of representatives interested in this subject, for preliminary discussion and formulation of plans. It was recommended by that meeting that a volume on the Church and the Jewish people should be prepared for publication under the leadership of Bishop Neill. A rough outline of the subjects that required to be treated was drawn up, and possible authors of the different chapters were recommended.

In the spring of 1951, however, Bishop Neill, owing to his other duties in the W.C.C., found it necessary to relinquish the responsibility for the projected volume, and I was asked to try to fulfil the plans already made.

As far as possible the outline recommended has been followed in this volume now being presented to the public. The editor confesses that he has failed to produce a genuinely corporate work, since the contributions constitute a series of more or less independent essays. But it is hoped that readers will find the volume truly objective and reliable. The volume is projected under Christian auspices and one of its chief purposes is to bring home to Christians their continuing responsibility in relation to the Jewish people of today. Because of this, not only Christians but also Jewish writers have been asked to contribute to the volume. This will also give added value to the discussions and action concerning the relations between the Churches and the Jewish people that are likely to be stimulated by this volume, both at the second Assembly of the W.C.C. in Evanston, August 1954, and in the Churches and parishes during years to come.

The volume was initiated under the auspices of the World Council of Churches but is now sponsored by the International Missionary Council's Committee on the Christian Approach to the Jews. It is hoped that it will serve the purpose of both the W.C.C. and the I.M.C. in its Evangelism and Missionary programme, and also be of help to many ministers of Churches and individual Christians in their relations to the Jews. It is also the wish of the editor that this book may serve to enlighten many Jews about Christianity today.

To all contributors to this 'symposium' the editor desires to extend his thanks. To the Publishing House, the Edinburgh House Press, the editor is indebted for good advice and valuable help in the production of the book.

GÖTE HEDENQUIST

# CONTENTS

# CONTRIBUTORS

Rabbi Dr Leo Baeck, London : before the war the Chief Rabbi of Berlin, Germany. In spite of his age (he was 80 in 1953) he is still teaching at the Hebrew Union College in Cincinnati, U.S.A., every winter term.

The Rev. W. A. Curtis, London : General Secretary of the Church Missions to Jews, London. Minister of the Church of England.

The Rev. H. L. Ellison, London : tutor at the London Bible College ; former tutor at the London College of Divinity and head of the Anglican Mission to Jews in Bukarest, Rumania ; Chairman of the Committee on Work among the Jews of the Conference of Missionary Societies in Great Britain and Ireland ; Executive member and former Vice-President of the International Hebrew Christian Alliance.

The Rev. Göte Hedenquist, Uppsala, Sweden : Director of the International Missionary Council's Committee on the Christian Approach to the Jews ; Minister of the Church of Sweden ; before the war leader of the Swedish Mission to Jews, Vienna, Austria ; 1946–50 Secretary in the Department of Reconstruction and Inter-Church Aid of the World Council of Churches in Geneva.

The Rev. Hans Kosmala, Jerusalem, Israel : Director of the Swedish Theological Institute in Jerusalem ; Minister of the Presbyterian Church of England ; former Director of die Institutum Delitzschianum in Leipzig and Vienna.

The Rev. Gösta Lindeskog, Uppsala, Sweden : Teol. Dr Docent of New Testament at the University of Uppsala ; Minister of the Church of Sweden ; autumn 1953, lecturer at the Swedish Theological Institute in Jerusalem ; Doctor's-thesis ' Die Jesusfrage im neuzeitlichen Judentum', 1938.

The Rev. R. Clephane Macanna, Edinburgh : Minister of the Church of Scotland and Secretary of its Overseas Department ; Chairman of the I.M.C.'s Committee on the Christian Approach to the Jews.

The Right Rev. Bishop Stephen Neill, D.D., World Council of Churches, Geneva : formerly Fellow of Trinity College, Cambridge ; Bishop of Tinnevelly, South India, 1939–1945.

The Rev. K. H. Rengstorf, D.D., Münster, Germany : Professor of Theology and Rector Magnificus of the University of Münster ; Minister of the Lutheran Church in Germany ; leader of the Institutum Delitzschianum, Münster ; Chairman of the German Evangelical Committtee for Service to Israel.

Dr Hans J. Schoeps, Erlangen, Germany : Professor of the history of religion at the University of Erlangen ; author of several important books on the relationship between the Jewish and Christian faiths and on the theology and history of Hebrew Christianity ; an outstanding representative of liberal Judaism of today.

The Rev. W. W. Simpson, London : General Secretary of the Council of Christians and Jews ; Minister of the Methodist Church in England.

The Rev. Robert Smith, Edinburgh : Minister of the Church of Scotland ; former missionary to the Jews in Prague, Czechoslovakia ; Editor of the *News Sheet*, organ of the I.M.C.'s Committee on the Christian Approach to the Jews.

# INTRODUCTION

STEPHEN NEILL

'I AM a Jew.' What is likely to be the reaction of the average Christian to this statement if made by an acquaintance not intimately known, by a fellow-traveller in the train, by the opposite number in a business deal? Perhaps the best description of his attitude is that he is likely to be *disconcerted*. Naturally, twentieth-century politeness will quickly and perhaps completely conceal the disturbance. After all, everyone knows that there are Jews in every country in the world, and that for the most part they are very normal and even likeable people. But there are deeper sub-conscious levels by which reactions are to some extent determined. And there the Christian, if he is quite honest, may find other motives, traditions, and racial memories at work. There is the element of fear : are not the Jews said to be a dangerously clever people, patient and penetrative, who have long been accustomed to find compensation for their oppressed condition by getting the better of the simple-minded Christian in a great variety of ways ? There is perhaps an unanalysable dislike. The traditional Western picture of the Jew—Shylock, Fagin, and so forth— has much more influence on the memory than such idealized presentations as Daniel Deronda. But perhaps deepest of all is a slight sense of discomfort, such as almost all men feel in the presence of the unknown, a discomfort which is often at the root of both fear and dislike. The Jew is mysterious ; he is the unknown ; he does not fit in.

If this is the Christian reaction, then the Christian is basically right. The Jew is a mystery ; he does not fit readily into any modern and Western categories. He is and remains an unassimilable element in the countries of his pilgrimage, in which through centuries of settlement he has never wholly ceased to be a pilgrim.

This is strange, and strangely disturbing. Jews have always been quick to adapt themselves to their situation. They have become loyal, and not infrequently eminent, citizens of their adopted countries.  In some wars they have joined up in the armies of conflicting Christian powers, and have fought against one another, not perhaps very deeply troubled by the logical incongruity of their position.  There is perhaps no position, other than that of king or queen, which has not been filled with distinction by a member of the Jewish race.   And yet they are never completely assimilable.   There is always in them something with which the Western world does not feel itself entirely at home.  The source of this something is not to be identified, as is sometimes done, with the fact that the Jews are still orientals.  *The true explanation of it is that the Jews have survived through centuries of persecution and oppression not as a race but as a religious group.*  By their faith they have lived, and it is still their faith that separates them from those who live about them.

There is, in reality, no such thing as a Christian nation or a Christian civilization.   Nevertheless it is true that the life of Europe has been penetrated through and through by Christian ideas, largely mediated through the minds of Greek Christian thinkers, and that even those who have repudiated or drifted away from the Christian faith cannot wholly get away from their own past.  Even Marxism has some claims to be considered a Christian heresy. Modern man in the West lives, or at least judges others, by an ethical code that represents a highly diluted form of Christian conviction.  Western philosophy is in origin and development, and even in the violent reactions against it, Christian philosophy.  By the Christian elements in this philosophy the development of modern science has been rendered possible and safeguarded.

To all this development and to all these influences the Jew is an alien.  Doubtless Jews who have been educated in Western schools and universities have come under these influences, which are indeed mediated even through such channels as the daily papers.  But it is religion that lays down the primary patterns of human existence, that creates those myths (to use contemporary sociological jargon) by which the general form of a society is determined. Worship and ritual, particularly as practised in the home—and Judaism even more than Christianity is a religion of the family and of the home—profoundly affect the outlook of each new generation as it grows up ; and this influence can continue for years and even for generations, even though the faithful practice of piety may have been lost. There are wide differences between the Christian Churches. But even the Christians who are most widely separated by doctrine, worship, and tradition are much more like one another than any of them is like the Jew. The division penetrates to the deepest levels of our being.

Perhaps the first feeling of a Christian who is brought much into contact with Jews is that the emotional structure of their being is determined by something immensely old. To what point in history do our conscious racial experiences go back? The date in history that every Englishman knows is 1066 ; and rightly, since 1066 does mark the beginning of modern England. The Swiss goes back instinctively to the formation of the League of the Four Cantons. American recollections usually reach back only to 1776, or perhaps by a stretch of imagination to the Pilgrim Fathers. As Christians, of course, we are well aware that we go back to Bethlehem and Calvary ; but our religious and our national life are not identical, in spite of the Christian penetration of our national life. If we are theologically well instructed, we are well aware of the continuity of the People of God in the Old and New Testaments, and we affirm with St Paul that Abraham is the father of our faith. But Abraham, Isaac, and Jacob are not continuously present to our thought. With the Jew it is otherwise. Unless he is wholly secularized, everything for him is determined by the sense of an unbroken continuity of four thousand years. The land, the book, the language, and the faith make up a four-fold cord that no change or vicissitude has ever been able to break. There are no gaps in Jewish history.

To the Christian of imagination who attends a synagogue service this becomes apparent immediately. The use of Hebrew speaks of something far older than the Greek or Latin of the Orthodox and Roman Catholic Churches. The chanting belongs to an age anterior to the development of Byzantine and Gregorian music. Everything expresses an age-old continuity, which even to the not very pious Jew is a living reality, and makes him almost a contemporary of Abraham. It is by such experiences, much more readily apprehended than expressed, that the character and outlook of a people are determined.

To the Christian who takes his religion seriously, the survival of the Jewish people is a mystery, a challenge, and a problem.

If there is any providential ordering of history—and, to the Christian, history is the sphere of the divine activity, in which the purposes of God are both revealed and brought to effect—the survival of the Jews is unintelligible except in relation to the providence of God. Contrary to all probability and expectation, this people, constantly persecuted and rejected, time and again face to face with total destruction, has nevertheless continued to exist, has multiplied, has spread itself abroad over the face of the earth, has succeeded in maintaining its essential unity—and such a phenomenon is so unusual in human history that in describing it we instinctively use the word ' miraculous '.

To those who accept the Christian revelation, the history of Israel, since its national rejection of the claims of Jesus of Nazareth to be the promised Messiah, presents itself as a history in parenthesis. This is not to deny the great significance of the Jewish experience across the centuries, or the value of Jewish thought, philosophical and ethical. But from the point of view of religious development, the pathetic words of Hosea have been all too literally fulfilled : ' The children of Israel shall abide many days without a king and without a prince, and without a sacrifice, and without an image, and without an ephod, and without teraphim.' It is within the sphere of the Christian Church, the new Israel, that progress in the knowledge of God has been made, and that revelation has been continuous. But a history in parenthesis is not a history that has come to an end : Christian thought at all times, though not universally, has recognized that, if Israel as a people has survived, it must be taken as probable that Israel as a people has still a great, perhaps a decisive, part to play in the consummation of the divine activity in history.

This is the problem with which St Paul is wrestling in the Epistle to the Romans. There are difficulties in the interpretation of his thought on the subject, but the main lines are clear enough. It is impossible that God should cast off His people : therefore Israel and the Church are both the People of God. Now they exist in separation. Yet this is not the last word : the future will see the reintegration of the separated parts. Israel will be brought back into the main stream of revelation. So all Israel shall be saved, and the restoration of its true position, the new unity between Jew and Gentile, will be as life from the dead.

Even Christians who hold firmly to St Paul's doctrine would hesitate to translate the glowing poetry of his vision into plain prose, or to bring eschatology into the realm of current history. Yet many of them would be inclined to hold, along the lines of this Pauline discussion, that, because of the separation between Church and synagogue, the People of God in some sense exists in a state of permanent schism. The divisions within the Christian Church are grave enough. But the gravest schism of all was the earliest, that which took place when Church and synagogue, not without mutual hostility and excommunication, decided to take their separate ways. Since that time one essential element in the life of the Church has been grievously lacking. The Church has indeed accepted the Old Testament as part of its sacred Scripture, has read and expounded and tried to understand it. But the main influence in the development of Christian thought was Greek. The debt of Western Christendom to the Greeks is immense, and almost all Christian thinking is carried on within the categories determined by the Greek Christian thinkers. But what came at the start as an illumination has tended to harden into an imprisonment ; the Greek categories are irrelevant or worse when the concern of the Church is to make itself at home in China, in India, or among primitive peoples. It may be that the difficulty the Church has certainly experienced in becoming a universal Church is in part due to the intellectualization of its thought under Greek influences, and that a large-scale recovery of the more direct, more concrete, more personal approach of the Hebrew mind is needed, if the Church is ever to fulfil its destiny as the spiritual home for all peoples.

It had long been the conviction of Christians who took a somewhat literal view of the Bible, and expected the literal fulfilment of Old Testament prophecy, that the Jews would return to Palestine ' in unbelief '. It is remarkable that this view should have been so firmly held at a time when Palestine seemed to be hopelessly and irrevocably under the Turkish yoke, and when such Jews as lived in Palestine were few, poor, and without influence in the land of their fathers. If a hundred years ago some student of prophecy had been inspired to set forth the astonishing series of events by which the State of Israel has come into being, he would have been dismissed as a foolish visionary ; a few improbabilities may be allowed to those who attempt to foresee the future, but he would have been accused of piling one improbability on another, and his study discredited. Yet all these improbabilities have come to pass within the space of little more than a generation of human life, and it is well that those who have long been interested in the Jewish problem should remind themselves of how little they foresaw of what has actually happened. It was taken for granted that the Jews were an unmilitary people, and that the fanatical valour which shines in the pages of Josephus had long been ground out of them by centuries of oppression. I must admit that, when some years ago a Jewish student assured me that the young men of the Haganah would ' simply eat up the Arabs ', I thought that he had allowed honourable patriotism to inhibit his common sense. But this was only one among the many miscalculations to be exposed by the astonishing course that events have actually taken.

The State of Israel has come into being. For the first time for centuries Jews have a home and a nationality of their own. Palestine today contains far more Jews than lived in it in the great days of Solomon. For the first time for centuries Jews in large numbers are living on the land and making the desert blossom as the rose.

It is already evident that the establishment of the State of Israel has not solved any problems, but has created a large crop of new ones. There is the continuing problem of the relations between Israel and the surrounding Arab states. There are considerable problems for Jews who have remained, and intend to remain, loyal citizens of the countries of their sojourning. The establishment of a political entity has not been entirely welcome to those who believe that religion and not politics has been and should be the essential factor in the survival of the Jewish people. There are the internal tensions of overcrowding, of an unstable economy, of the development of political insti-tutions for a people whose members have inherited diverse political traditions or none at all. There is the problem of many and varied attitudes towards Judaism, ranging from conservative acceptance of all the traditions to a radical repudiation of almost everything in the Jewish religious tradition.

But among the most serious problems of all is that of the future of Judaism, if Palestine one day becomes a wholly Jewish country, and if the Temple is restored to Jewish hands. What is Judaism today, and what can it become? Is the worship of the Temple to be restored on the ancient lines? Is sacrifice again to become its central act? To the Christian of the new Israel the problem does not present itself. It seems to him natural that the ordinances of sacrifice should have continued up till the time of Christ, since they were accepted in the ethnic as well as in the Jewish world. Oxen were led forth lowing to the skies, as they are immortalized in Keats' 'Ode on a Grecian Urn'. It was natural that the people of Lystra, mistaking

2

Paul and Barnabas for gods, should prepare to honour them with sacrifice. But to the Christian it is equally natural that, once the full, perfect, and sufficient sacrifice had been offered once for all in the body of Jesus Christ, the whole sacrificial organization of religion should be relegated to the past as having no longer significance in the present. It had in fact always belonged to the shadow and not to the substance, to the sign and not to the reality. And now that the reality has come, it is seen as part of that which already in the days of Jesus was growing old and was ready to vanish away. But can Judaism undergo any such spiritualization of its order without ceasing to be itself? Of necessity Judaism in exile has existed without sacrifice and offering; but there has never been agreement that the ordinances have been changed or abolished. If Judaism is once more at home in the city of David, if at some time in the future the ancient holy places come again into its hands, what will be its answer to the questions that at that time it will be impossible to evade? It is almost unthinkable that the order of sacrifice should be restored. But what is the alternative? For the moment, the question is not urgent. Nevertheless it is the duty of Christians to ask this question gently and persistently of their Jewish friends. In attempting to find the answer to the question, Judaism may be led to a profound rediscovery of its own true self.

In the meantime, there are many matters that belong to the realm not of theory but of practice. The existence of the State of Israel has brought home the Jewish problem to innumerable Christians with new force. It is evident that all Christians, even those who are not directly in touch with Jews, ought to know something about the problem, and ought to arrive at some conclusions as to what their Christian principles demand of them in this situation. Antisemitism is by no means dead, though in most countries happily at least dormant. Christians should be aware of the danger, and prepared to take measures in advance to guard against its recrudescence.

It may be said with confidence that most Christians are unaware of the shameful record of Christendom in the past in relation to the Jews, and that there has never been anything like an adequate and concerted repentance on the part of Christendom for these old wrongs. Corporate repentance is an idea not easily susceptible of theological analysis, and hypocrisy very easily enters in when men are invited to repent of sins in which they had no share and of which their individual consciences are entirely clear. Yet every churchman shares in a measure in responsibility for the action of the Church, and also for its negligences and ignorances. As Christians we ought to know how often the Church has been grievously compromised by its complicity in persecution ; how often, in spite of such examples as the heroic witness and actions of countless churchmen in the days of the Nazi persecution of the Jews, the Churches as a whole have failed to make their voice effectively heard on behalf of the oppressed. Knowledge of these things leads to a due sense of humility in relation to the past, and also of responsibility for the future.

The guilt of Christendom is so heavy that it can hardly be exaggerated. But it must also be remembered that, in any matter of human controversy, guilt is rarely if ever wholly concentrated on one side, and that, if better relations are to prevail between Jews and Christians, Jews also are called to repentance and to a sense of responsibility. Jews are rather too easily led into the error of supposing that, because of their relative innocence, they may claim total innocence in the field of Jewish-Gentile relationships. Their warmest friends are sometimes exasperated by the way in which Jews through lack of moderation make it difficult for their friends to plead their cause.

Where there has been tension, strife, or conflict, it is only on the basis of penitence and forgiveness that the parties can meet with any hope of bringing into being a new order of mutual trust and goodwill. Penitence makes possible a total frankness of expression and discussion, which again is indispensable as a foundation for lasting goodwill. It is perfectly true that one of the first results of an unfamiliar frankness is likely to be mutual exasperation. The tendency to self-defence (of which true penitence is the denial) is so strong in all of us that it is hard to see our own position as it presents itself to another, and to bear patiently with his point of view, when the admixture of injustice and prejudice, inseparable from all human attitudes, is all too plainly seen in it.  But this stage has to be passed through, and no permanently useful results are attained where a false politeness masks deep underlying differences of feeling or conviction.  We begin to be useful to one another when we can say gently but fearlessly what we really believe, and when we can bear the frank expression of another's views without rancour or offence.

Much frank discussion between Jews and Christians is needed.  But there is a danger of sterility in discussion which leads on to nothing except further discussion.  It is greatly to be desired that mutual understanding should lead on to co-operation in all those many fields in which Jews and Christians can work together in perfect mutual confidence. The agencies which exist are doing commendable work, and ought to be multiplied.  But it is desirable that they should not too narrowly limit their field of activity. Wherever there are signs of a renewal of racial or religious intolerance, Christians and Jews must close their ranks firmly and stand together against the danger.  But, apart from this somewhat negative attitude, there are many positive contributions to be made in the modern world. Jews and Christians are agreed as to human rights and liberties, as to the obligation resting on all men of goodwill to strive ceaselessly for the establishment and maintenance of peace.  In many communities, co-operation in such matters as housing and the care of the young is an obvious possibility.  On all such matters Jewish-Christian agreement is much deeper than a politic or opportunist willingness to sink differences.  The common religious heritage of Jews and Christians in the Old Testament has provided them with common standards of judgment and of reference, and a common range of ethical convictions which can be taken for granted as a foundation for action in fellowship.

Yet here at once a caution has to be entered against taking this common ground to be wider than it actually is.

Jews and Christians both read and honour the Old Testament, but they do not read and honour it in the same way.
To the Christian the Old Testament is not simply a collection
of old historical records : it is a living voice of prophecy
which speaks to him of Jesus Christ.  The whole book has
been reread and reinterpreted in the light of Him who
has come, and to whom the Christian sees it as pointing.
The principle of interpretation is now Christological.  This
is true of all Christians, not only of those who claim specially
to hold to the Christological principle, and the eccentricities
of whose interpretation are sometimes as difficult for other
Christians to accept as they would be for Jews.  God is
still the God of Abraham, Isaac, and Jacob ; but He is
that God as seen revealed in the face of the One whose day
Abraham rejoiced to see.  He is still the God who at the
creation said, 'Let there be light', but that God as known
through the light that is in the face of Jesus Christ.  There
is hardly a passage in the Old Testament that is not affected
by this revaluation.

Christians cannot, of course, expect to impose their
judgment and their interpretations on their Jewish brethren.
This point has been made simply to guard against the
possibility of illusion.  We use the same words, but we do
not always use them in the same way.  We sometimes
appear to be agreed when apparent agreement covers
deep division.  If we are honestly aware of where we differ,
we can co-operate without misunderstanding ; if we fail
to realize the differences, there is likely to come a moment
of sore disillusionment and bitterness.

There is one point at which it is essential that Jews and
Christians should understand one another.  Christianity is
a missionary religion, and it can never be anything else.  It
is the conviction of Christians that Christ died for all, and
that this Gospel is to be preached to all nations, to the Jew
first and also to the Greek.  On this point no compromise
of any kind is possible.  If Christianity ceases to be in
principle a universal religion, it is no longer Christianity.
If co-operation is offered on the understanding that ' propaganda ' and ' proselytism ' are barred, the Christian cannot

accept co-operation on those terms. To do so would be a denial of something which he honestly believes. This does not mean that the Christian is committed to intemperate and irritating propaganda, in season and out of season ; what he cannot accept is the position of appearing to have denied himself the possibility of Christian witness, when it is in season.

This characteristic of the Christian religion is an offence, not only to the Jew but also to the Hindu and to the Moslem. But who ever imagined that the Gospel could be anything other than an offence ? Certainly not Jesus of Nazareth, who spoke again and again of the offence that He was bringing into the world. It is well that this offence should be plainly recognized and stated by Christians ; concealment and compromise can only do harm, and, if we are to work together, we must know plainly where we are.

Christian propaganda among their people is most strenuously objected to by Jews. In part there is good ground for their objections. At times Christian missionary effort has really been proselytism in the worst sense of the term. Pressure has been exercised by governments, even to the extent of the denial of the most elementary human rights. Advantage has been taken of the poverty of Jews to bring mercenary considerations to bear in aid of what has pretended to be merely the preaching of the Gospel. Undue influence has been exercised on young people, who could not well know their own minds, and unbearable divisions have been created in families and in communities.

It is essential that Christian Churches and individual Christians interested in fellowship with the Jews should repudiate once for all, and from the heart, every method which in the light of the Gospel and of the ordinary human conscience must be condemned. Honesty, charity, sincerity, and a profound respect for the convictions of others are the only basis on which a Christian approach can be made to those of other faiths. Where any of these necessary conditions is lacking, contact between Christians and those of other faiths can only do harm. The Christian bearing witness to his faith needs constantly to look at things from the other man's point of view, to understand and to sympathize with objections which in the last resort he cannot regard as well founded.

But here again repentance is demanded of both parties and not only of one. The Jew too has to be asked to consider again his attitude to the witness of those of other faiths than his own.

The Declaration of Human Rights includes a number of clauses concerning religious liberty ; among the rights which it is intended to secure is that of a man to change his religious profession, if he becomes honestly convinced of the truth of a religion other than that in which he has been brought up. There are many conversions from motives that will not for a moment bear the light of day. But equally there are conversions, in all directions, that bear upon them the most evident marks of sincerity. Jews and Christians alike, if they desire to make a stand for religious liberty, must face honestly all the implications of the right of free enquiry and free decision in matters of religion.

There has been a tendency for Jews to condemn every Jew who has ever become a Christian as a renegade, as a traitor to his people. This attitude must be wholly given up. A man who from sincere conviction has made the sacrifice of giving up the traditions in which he has been reared, and of separating himself from his own kindred and people, deserves and should receive the respect that is the due of an honest man, and not least from those who most disagree with the step that he has taken. Christians are not pleased when one among their number becomes a Moslem or a Buddhist ; but in such circumstances they are called to exercise just such patience in judgment and such respect for sincere conviction as is demanded of the Jews in relation to one of their number who has become a Christian convert.

Conversely, it must be recognized that the Jews have every right to bear witness to their faith and to try to win others for it. On the whole Judaism in the centuries of oppression has not developed the universalist tendencies which are clearly expressed in the second part of the prophecy of Isaiah ; the Jews have been content rather to guard the law for themselves than to think of it as a universal law going forth from Zion to be a blessing and a guide to the Gentiles also. But if, with greater liberty and influence open to them, they feel led to proclaim their way as God's sole revelation for Jew and Gentile alike, and to open the door for proselytes as they did in the days of Jesus and Paul, no one should attempt to say them Nay—provided of course that this propaganda is conducted fairly, and only on a basis of religious and spiritual conviction.

Of the sincere Christian it is demanded by his faith that in relation to the Jews he should not consider that his duty has been fulfilled by the exercise of tolerance and fair-mindedness. It is required of him that he desire under-standing, deep sympathy, and even affection for the people of Israel. This volume is dedicated to the promotion of understanding. That it will serve its purpose for those who read it carefully can hardly be doubted. But it is to be hoped that for many Christian readers it will be only a beginning, and will stimulate the desire for personal contact and for a deeper understanding from within of all that is best in the life and traditions of Judaism. I can hardly imagine any better method for the pursuit of this aim than that a Christian should obtain a copy of the standard Jewish Prayer Book, Hebrew and English, and should study it in detail. After all, a religion can be understood only in its life of worship. To the Christian reader much of the Jewish liturgy will be familiar through its use of the Old Testament. But there will be other prayers which are unfamiliar, and which will speak to his heart, through their dignity, through their sense of vocation and of fidelity to vocation, through their poignant accents of hope and expectation. When we have entered into the spirit of the prayers, we may hope to be able to begin to understand the people.

Finally, the Christian is called to exercise towards the Jewish people, and towards those Jews whom he may happen to meet, the love which the Saviour showed and shows towards them. The attitude of many Christians towards Israel has been fatally prejudiced by memories of the terrible cry of the people on the day of the Crucifixion, ' His blood be on us and on our children '. The blood of the Innocent has been associated with judgment, with vengeance and a curse, as though God had finally cast off His people. As we have seen, this is not true. It was the blood of Abel that pleaded for vengeance, but the blood of Jesus speaketh better things than that of Abel (Heb. xii : 24). This blood of sprinkling is the blood of the new covenant ; it speaks of ransom, of forgiveness, of cleansing, of acceptance. It is this blood that is sprinkled on Jews and Gentiles alike. It is true that for Israel as a people this word of pardon has not yet become generally effective. Through the long parenthesis of Israel's history since the day of the Crucifixion, it might seem that the people had been forgotten. But if in truth Christ died for all, then this people also is sealed and signed with the mark of the divine pardon, this people also is called to inherit the new covenant no less than the old. Israel is beloved both for the fathers' sakes and for his own. The Christian who has realized these truths cannot fail to join with deep sincerity and affection in the exclamation of St Paul : ' My heart's desire and prayer to God for Israel is that they may be saved '.

# THE JEWISH PROBLEM AND THE CHURCH'S UNDERSTANDING OF ITS OWN MISSION

## Karl Heinrich Rengstorf

### I

THE fact that the Jewish people still exists after so many centuries and has outlived most of its foes makes it one of the greatest riddles for the historian. But even more than for the historian it is a cause of wonder for the Christian observer.

Jesus came first to the lost sheep of the house of Israel, to His own people, that He might fulfil the promise given to Israel. But His people rejected Him. His people did not accept the witness of the Apostles. And the result of this was that, while their witness spoke of the fulfilling of the times in Jesus as the Messiah of Israel, the Church of this Jesus grew up as a Church of the Gentiles. So, today, the Jews and the Church of Jesus exist apart from each other, His people and His Church. Both appeal to the authority of God's prophetic promise ; but while the Church says that the Jews stand outside the salvation which has come, the Jews maintain the view that it was one of the most ill-fated moments in the history of mankind when a few enthusiastic disciples of Jesus felt themselves obliged to proclaim their Master, not merely as one of the greatest of their Teachers, perhaps the greatest of them all, but as the promised Messiah of their people.

Here is the beginning of a number of theological problems which are presented to the Church by the existence and the form of the Jewish people *post Christum natum*. Over them all lies the shadow of the Cross. The Church would not be true to itself, and would not truly represent its view of the Jewish people and their character, if this fact were not kept constantly in mind in considering the Jewish problem and in discussion with Jews.

Thus in what follows the attempt is made to deal with the problem which the Jews raise for the Church, to regard it and to deal with it as a problem of the Church itself, whose solution is to be found in the Cross of Jesus and in that alone. This affects the method of the investigation. The Holy Scriptures of both Testaments will be studied from the point of view of the Jews and from the point of view of the Church. If the Bible is really a single whole, this must be shown in the answer which is obtained, in so far as the right answer will not, in the first place, justify the Church, but rather present it with a task. But let us examine the problems.

II

## A. ELECTION AND REDEMPTION

(i) Whenever anyone makes the attempt to determine the historical position of either Judaism or the Christian Church, he can have only one legitimate starting-point. It is to be found in that event which the Bible describes as the election of the descendants of Abraham by God, the Creator of Heaven and Earth, and the Ruler of the World and of the nations, to be the people of His choice. This event, which came about (in a miraculous way after a long preparation from the days of Abraham on, and as part of a fixed divine plan) at Sinai, the place of the revelation of the Will of God to all the World, is seen throughout the Holy Scriptures of the Old and New Testaments as that historic act of God without which there would have been no salvation for the whole of mankind. It will be expressly noticed that the New Testament includes here everything that it has to say about the salvation entrusted to the Church of Jesus Christ (cf. only Rom. ix–xi in the whole of the Epistle to the Romans). This fact has the inevitable consequence for Judaism and the Church, when they enter into discussion with each other, that they come into a very remarkable and real partnership.   Certainly the Church on the one hand cannot see and understand its mission unless it constantly keeps in mind the Old Testament and what it records.   But on the other hand the Jews can only explain their existence and their right by reference to the New Testament and the history to which it gives witness.   This is simply the consequence of the fact that the Church of Jesus Christ from the beginning appropriated as its own the claim of the Old Testament congregation.   Unlike Judaism, the Church cannot distinguish between the salvation which is bound up with the fellowship of Abraham and the salvation which Jesus Christ secures.   This is the reason why Judaism can never speak frankly of its meaning for the salvation of the world without mentioning also Christianity and its claim.

(ii) In this the New Testament stands alongside the Old Testament, for it concedes to the Jews that their election by God gives them not only their existence, but also a unique and lasting dignity (Matt. xxi : 33 ff. ; Luke xiii : 16 ; xix : 9 ;  John viii : 37 ;  Rom. xi : 28 ;  etc.).   For this very reason it is important that the Church also bases its dignity and the dignity of its members on the divine election. This election, however, does not coincide with the election of Israel.   For the New Testament it lies in time long before the hour of God on Sinai.   Indeed, it lies before all time : namely, in that eternal decree of God's love which was revealed in Jesus Christ (I Thess. i : 4 ;  I Cor. i : 26 ff.) and which results in our belonging to Him in faith and baptism (I Cor. i : 30 etc.).   From the New Testament standpoint one must even say that the election effective in the Church, the election in Jesus Christ, is a presupposition of the election of Israel for the salvation of the World.   The election in Jesus Christ does not, therefore, follow the election of Israel at Sinai as a second act of God : rather, the election of Israel at Sinai is the consequence of the eternal decree of God's love from all eternity.

(iii) For the New Testament, however, the election which

is effective for and in the Church precedes that of Israel not only in time, but also in content.   For in the New Testament, election in Jesus Christ is, at the same time, redemption. For the New Testament, God, by the election in His Son and by the redemption bestowed through Him, realizes what He has ordained in the election of Israel, His promise concerning the Old Testament people of God (cf. Rom. iv : 1 ff. ;  v : 1 f.).   In this connection we must not overlook the fact that, for the Old Testament too, the election of Israel has as its goal the redemption of the Gentiles as well.

(iv) In view of this one might expect that the New Testament Church would feel itself superior to Israel.   But that is not the case.   On the contrary, though the New Testament Church is conscious of the certainty of being elected in a higher sense than Israel, this is linked, not with the consciousness of superiority, but with a deep sorrow. This sorrow springs from the knowledge that the Jews as such, although chosen by God, have not yet come to the goal which was appointed with their election, but are still excluded from it.   Here we may refer to the words of Jesus as well as to the witness of Paul, the Apostle to the Gentiles—being himself of the seed of Abraham (cf. Matt. viii : 11 f. ;  xxiii : 37 ff. ;  Luke xix : 41 ff. ;  above all, Rom. ix : 1 ff.).

(v) The exceptional position of the Church which results from this finds its expression in two ways.   On the one hand, the Church understands itself to be the real or spiritual Israel, and as such regards the heavenly Jerusalem as her city (Gal. iv : 26 ;  Phil. iii : 20 ;  etc., especially Rev.). On the other hand, however, the sacred title of Israel is still granted to the Jews, although they lack the sign of the true Israel, which is faith without reserve ; it is not of very great consequence that in the records preserved to us the title is used only where the context raises the question of ' election and redemption ' (cf. Rom. ix–xi and Phil. iii : 5). Besides this, the situation of the Church is expressed in the fact that the early Christian universalism, even in the person of its most outspoken representative, the Apostle Paul, has never lost sight of one thing :  the call to Faith through the Gospel is ' to the Jew first ', and this cannot be altered even by the sharpest Jewish opposition.   Here lies the last and deepest reason for the fact that the Church, so long as it is a Church composed only of Gentiles, feels itself to be incomplete (Rom. xi : 16 ff. ;  cf. also Ephes. ii : 11 ff.).   The Church of God in Jesus Christ, in its origin as well as in its nature, in its own eyes and in the eyes of the world, is the Church of both Jews and Gentiles.   It ceases to be the people of God when it forgets or denies this.   Thus it comes about that the Church is unfaithful to itself, as the work of the eternal divine election, when it does not constantly pray for the redemption of the Jewish people as the people of the Old Testament election.   Indeed, one must even say that the Church rightly understands itself as the one universal Church of the divine salvation only when it prays for the Jewish people with deep sorrow and with earnest longing.

## B. THE LAW AND THE SPIRIT

(i) What distinguishes the Jewish people from all other peoples is the Law, which according to the Old Testament record God Himself gave to His people on Mount Sinai in the hour of election.   God's Law, the Torah, places the Jewish people in a unique and peculiar way under the will of God.   It is notable that the interest here is not so much in the individual members of the people as in the people as a whole, as a community, as a nation.   It is only by belonging to the people of the Law that an individual man becomes a Jew, as a man under the Law.   Thus it would be false to assume that Israel is a people of the Law because all its members keep the Law.   It is only because this is not the case that proselytes can share in all the blessings promised to the chosen people and the people of the Law.

The absolute validity of the Divine Will in the Law— the sovereignty of God, the theocracy—is realized in the worship which shapes the whole life of the Jewish people in all its members according to definite rules.   Therefore the Jews have always been bound to separate themselves strictly from all those of their members who transgress the Law or seek to escape it. For a pious descendant of Abraham and even for a pious proselyte there can be no fellowship with one who despises or transgresses the Law. Every offence against the Law is necessarily not only an offence against God's Will, and so a profanation of God and of His Name, but also a desecration of the people chosen by God and subject to His Will.

(ii) This subjection of the Jewish people to God's revealed will makes the holiness, which results from their separation from the nations, practically dependent on their own conduct, that is on their obedience to the Will of God in the Law. In the instructions of the Law it is therefore expressly emphasized again and again how important it is that the Will of God should really be done (and correspondingly in the New Testament—Matt. xix : 17 ; Rom. ii : 17 ff. ; Gal. iii : 12). Thus it is appropriate that the prophetic criticisms of Israel—just like Jesus' criticism of the righteous ones of His people—start with the practice of the Law, that is with obedience or disobedience. Whether Israel is the ' Holy People' (Deut. vii : 6), whether it is ' My People' or ' not My People ' (Hos. ii : 1 ff.) depends for the prophets, just as for Jesus, and also for John the Baptist and for Paul, on whether the Jews as a people do the will of God in His Law or not, and whether they as a people follow His call in an unlimited obedience or fail Him in this.

(iii) The Church too understands itself as holy, as *sancta ecclesia*. Since its first beginning this title has expressed the fact that the Church can only understand itself as the work of God. ' Holy ' means in the language of the New Testament ' sanctified by God ', but the Church also knows that God's will is valid for it, that His will is sanctification, the sanctification of all its members without exception (I Thess. iv : 3 and v : 18). The Church, however, unlike Israel, finds its holiness not conditioned by its conduct. It lives by the Holy Spirit : that is, the Spirit of God as well as of its Lord Jesus Christ. The Church is the fruit of His working. Therefore for the Church there is no more appropriate description of itself than the title of the ' Body of Christ '. This New Testament title leaves no doubt that the sanctification of the individual Christian takes place only within the sanctification of the Church by the Holy Spirit (cf. I Cor. vii : 14 ; Rom. xi : 16 ; and the ' House Tables '). This is connected with the fact that the New Testament does not know anything that might be called ' individual ethics ', but only ' community ethics '. In this respect the Church is in no way different from Judaism of all periods from the beginning to the present day.

(iv) From this standpoint it proves impossible to make the distinction between the Church and the Jewish people, as the people of the divine election and of the divine will, that in Judaism all the weight lies on the community, while in the Church, on the other hand, all weight lies on the individual. If anything is utterly false, it is this distinction. The fact is rather that, just as the individual Christian in his decision of faith repeats the decision of the first Christian generation and of the Church, and makes it his own, so also he acts, in so far as he acts obediently and in a Christian way, always as ' *pars pro toto* ', that is as a member of his community. In this respect, therefore, there is no difference in principle between the Church and Judaism. It corresponds to this similarity of principle between Israel and the Church, that the Commandment of God on Mount Sinai, the Decalogue, has been made the foundation of Christian social life. In the nature of things it cannot be otherwise. But this has considerable consequences. It follows necessarily from this that the boundary between the Church and Judaism does not run in the sphere of ethics, and cannot run in that sphere. It runs in the sphere of faith, and it becomes visible in the way of seeing and comprehending God.

(v) Leo Baeck has rightly and very impressively emphasized that, in a time when all religious life is endangered by secularism, the Jewish principle of the relentless Divine imperative, ' Thou shalt ', is an extraordinarily important factor in the spiritual and cultural situation of the world. This judgment must remain true, even if this principle were one day to be manifest in no other way than this : that there were Jews who traced their existence and their

3

character to this principle, without drawing all the consequences from it.   In any case, Christianity can only bow
with reverence when this principle is met with in a Jew, or
in a Jewish community, as a way of life.   For it comes face
to face with the reflection of that dignity, which God
Himself gave to the Jewish people when He chose them and
revealed His will to them.   Thus the Church has no right
to call this dignity of Israel an anachronism and simply to
ignore it.   God has not abolished this dignity to this very
day.   The Church and its members will understand and
judge this dignity rightly only when they appreciate what
is their special gift, beyond the obligation to obedience,
in the endowment with the Holy Spirit of God through
Jesus Christ.   Therefore, the Church will understand its
own dignity rightly only if, by the sight of the dignity
which has been given to Israel, it is constantly stimulated
to be in all appearance what it already understands itself
to be in all its members : Christ's Body, God's new creation,
the fellowship of those people who in spite of all human
failure have been powerfully renewed in Christ through the
Spirit of God (II Cor. v : 17).

## C. SUFFERING AND HOPE

(i) The history of Israel is that of a people subject to
suffering from the beginning.   This is connected with the
fact that the peoples of the world feel strange and uncomfort-
able whenever they are confronted with the people of the
divine election.

But the suffering of Israel has a further explanation,
even more important than the first, resulting from the
separation of Israel from the nations.   This further explanation arises from the fact that God has always been compelled by the unfaithfulness of His people to punish them
in order to train them.   In this way it is noticeable that
the tension with the nations of the world is reflected within
the people themselves : in the tension between its pious
and its godless members who hate the pious of their own
people.

(ii) Thus the Jewish people and suffering belong together. The knowledge of this fact accompanies them even in the pre-Christian period. Probably this is the explanation of the remarkable veil of mystery which lies over the figure of the Suffering Servant of God in Deutero-Isaiah. It cannot be decided with certainty whether this figure has to be understood collectively, as a personification of the people of Israel, or as a definite individual person. Some-thing can be said for both views, but neither solution is altogether satisfactory. The cause of this lies not in the commentators, but in the subject with which the prophet is concerned. Over it lies the divine mystery, that election and suffering belong together for Israel and for its members. Thus it is the result of the special Providence and experience of the Jewish people, when outstanding spiritual leaders of modern Judaism like Leo Baeck are inclined to see the historical mission of the Jews in this very thing, that they suffer time and again in obedience to their election and as representatives of the Divine Will, and that in their suffering they witness to the God of Israel's election as the God of History, the Lord of all the World.

(iii) Closely connected with the destiny of suffering which results from its separation from the nations, there is a radiant hope of the future which runs through the whole history of the Jewish people. It culminates in the certainty that God will finally lead His people through all suffering to glory. He will give His people a share in His own glory when He reveals it at the end of the days before the nations. It is extraordinarily impressive to see how all through this history the certainty runs, that God Himself will justify the existence and the character of His people in this way before the whole world, and will show the greatness of its achievement as the people of the Divine Will. But it is most impressive of all that this certainty shines most radiantly when the Jewish people seem at last to be doomed to extinction. The greater their distress, the more certain they are of God's final victory, which will bring with it the honourable exaltation of His chosen people.

(iv) In view of this we cannot evade the question whether

Zionism and the establishment of a Jewish State in Palestine
is not a departure from this self-understanding of Judaism and
a ' break-away ' from the path indicated by God, and thus
an abandonment of the Biblical line in its judgment about
itself.  Now it is certain that both Zionism itself, and still
more the Jewish State which it has established, result
from the endeavour to withdraw Judaism from the constant
menace of the nations of the world, above all from this
menace in its two classical forms, in antisemitism and in
assimilation.  One must, however, say that the New Israeli
State, whatever it has achieved, has certainly not ended
the dispersion of the Jews among the nations, the Galuth,
and so it has not ended the constant menace to the Jews
through the nations.  Even if all the Jews in the world were
to return to Palestine, this would not mean the restoration
of that people of God which between 70 and 135 A.D. lost
its Statehood, its theocratic constitution, its worship, and
its home.

One can already say today that there will be in the
future, not only an exile (Galuth) as before, but also that
the exile-existence of the Jewish people will be continued
in Palestine.  This will, of course, take place in a quite new
form of exile : namely, not in an outward but in a spiritual
exile.  The clock of history cannot be put back.  Further,
the Jewish people when it now comes ' home ', can never
be at home in its former and newly won homeland, as it
was at home there before the beginning of the great exile,
and before the suffering which went with it.

(v) In practice the position is this, that the *Christus
natus*, in a way no one would have considered possible
before, now proves to be the criterion also for the new
way of the Jewish people.  This is the case in so obvious a
way that the Church has no need to proclaim it to the Jews
in any programme or propaganda.  This knowledge should
prevent the Church from feeling that it is bound to state
its attitude to the modern establishment of the Jewish State
in the form of a theological recommendation.  Here we
cannot go thoroughly into the problem.  But so much must
be clear from what has been said, that the Church is engaged

in a very dangerous venture if it makes any attempt to interpret what is happening in Israel, because this is beyond its vision.

Taking a theological attitude to the establishment of the Jewish State is, on the contrary, a matter for the Jews themselves. It will ultimately hinge on the question of the Messiah. At the same time, the question of their attitude to the ' *Christus natus* ' of the Church's faith is one that cannot be evaded. Whether and when and how this will be decided it is useless to speculate. At present the probability is that the broadest circles especially of Israeli Jewry do not intend to bring this question into their discussions on the law and life of the young State.

The Church has every ground to acquiesce in this. As a result of events in Palestine it has one more opportunity to show and prove that it is not only a believing Church but also a waiting Church. Only as such can it keep on the right lines with regard to the Jewish people, the lines on which it has been set by the Lord Himself, and by His Apostles, and above all by the Apostle Paul.

(vi) For the general situation and its Christian interpretation what is happening at present in Palestine—surely not without God's guidance—may be less important than something quite different. The important thing is that in our times the Church too throughout the whole world is coming to recognize, to an extent which must be unheard of since its beginning, that it is destined for suffering in this world and in this time. In the whole world both old and young Churches are beginning to confirm this recognition anew in their own suffering.

It goes without saying that the Church rightly sees in such suffering the effect of its communion with its Lord, who is the Crucified. This is the fulfilment of the prospect for the Church which Jesus, face to face with His own way of suffering and death, promised His disciples for the sake of their relationship with Him.

(vii) Besides this it must not be overlooked that in the self-understanding of Christianity there is gaining ground at present another notion, which has also been of the highest importance for the self-understanding of the Jews at all times. This is the recognition that the Church too cannot exist in this time and in this world except in the form of a Diaspora. This idea is thoroughly familiar and current in the New Testament (Gal. iv : 26 ; Phil. iii : 20 ; Hebr. *passim*). Naturally, this view is connected with the position of the Old Testament People of God among the nations of the world, as described by the word ' Galuth '.

It can hardly be a coincidence that the idea of the Diaspora-character of Christianity is once more becoming alive at a time when persecution and exile are the lot of the Church in many places. But it is also very remarkable that this is happening while at the same time the classical people of the Galuth, the Jewish people, is engaged, not without apparent success, in an endeavour to put an end to its own Diaspora-existence and to the dangers that go with it. Here if anywhere the finger of God may be indicating to Jews and to Christians both what they have in common and where they differ.

(viii) Suffering and dispersion as a feature of the life of the Church result from the fact that the Church is the Church of Jesus Christ. Now Jesus Christ is for the Church the Risen, Exalted One, the One who is to come, and that, not in spite of, but because of the fact that He is the Crucified One. In the Cross of Jesus the Church recognizes and confesses the act of God, which is decisive for history as the history of God's dealings with the world. At the same time it is conclusive for the Church that this act of God appears as an act of obedience and trust by Jesus Christ in fulfilment of the will of God as His Father.

It is the very Cross, therefore, which provides the Church with the proof that God will achieve His goal, the revelation of His righteousness before the world and over the world. When Jesus went to the Cross and suffered death He completed that perfect surrender to the will of God which was the purpose of the election of the descendants of Abraham, and which summed up the meaning of the revelation of God's will in His Law (Deut. vi : 5 ff.). The fulfilling of the will of God in the complete surrender of Jesus is the way in which God has glorified Himself.  The death of Jesus on the Cross thus vindicates and gives profound and final meaning to the suffering and exile which the Church shares with its Lord in the time between His coming in the flesh and His coming again in glory (cf. on this point also Matt. viii : 20 ;  Luke xiii : 33).

(ix) For the relationship of the Church to the Jews the result of all this is, first of all, a far-reaching similarity as regards the external situation.  This arises from the peculiar position of both within history, and it necessarily affects the self-understanding both of the Jews and of the Church alike.  It does not matter in this connection that the historical position of the Church and of the Jews is not the same, and that therefore their motives in their respective situations in the world do not coincide.  If the Church is clear that this is in fact the state of affairs—and the Church must be clear about this, if it is or wishes to be the Church of Jesus Christ—then it follows logically that there must be a genuine and deep solidarity between the Church and the Jewish people in respect to the situation of the Jews in the world.  It is high time that the Church began to witness in an appropriate way to this solidarity with the Jews and to make it visible and audible.  For this solidarity of the situation is the most effective sign ordained by God for the Jews in and with the Church.

It is therefore a grievous hindrance in Jewish–Christian relationships that hitherto the Church, if it has noticed this solidarity at all, has almost always denied it, or at least not confessed it.  In this solidarity, which has nothing to do with sentimentality or with humanitarian philo-Judaism, but which may be learnt from Paul (cf. para. iv ; p. 30), lies the decisive factor—because it is inherent in the nature of Judaism and of the Church—which will make possible such an encounter of the Jews with the Church of Jesus Christ as will prevent them from evading it or its witness without denying themselves.  On the other hand, without this solidarity the Jewish people can never and will never recognize the way of the Church, far less walk in it, as the way in which their own destiny, so full of grace and of bitterness, is fulfilled and reaches its goal.   Perhaps one must go so far as to say : If the Jews in the last hundred years have gone the way of political self-redemption, we must see in this first of all the consequences of grave guilt on the part of the Church.   The Church has incurred this guilt, however, because it has not placed itself in a genuine solidarity of suffering and ' Galuth ' with Israel, following its crucified and risen Lord.

## D. Justice and Love

(i) In the picture of the Old Testament tradition the election of Israel coincides with the establishment of God's Covenant with His people.   Through the Covenant Israel is bound to God and under obligation to Him.   The Covenant also excludes the possibility that Israel might separate itself from God.

In this way the Covenant of God with His people is the condition not only of the promises which were given to Israel as God's chosen people, but also of the preaching and judgment of repentance to the people through the ages, beginning with Moses, and continuing with the preaching of the Prophets, and so on until John the Baptist, and the word of repentance with which Jesus took up the preaching of the Baptist and brought it to an end.

(ii) While the election of Israel is the work of Divine Grace, through the Covenant which God has established with Israel it has come under Divine Law.   This sentence is in no way limited by the fact that according to the Law (Deut. vi : 5) it is the love of God which shall determine the relationship of the people and all its members to God at every moment and in every situation.   On the contrary, the way in which the Commandment of Love was under-stood and fulfilled at the time of Jesus, or even the death of Akiba, who died with the words of the so-called Schma' (Deut. vi : 4 f.) on his lips, shows that the love of God was more and more understood and practised as something which was demanded by God.

(iii) While here, in His encounter with men and also in

the gracious choice of the descendants of Abraham as a people peculiar to God, the righteousness of God, which determines all His actions, is shown as the righteousness which demands, the New Testament understands the righteousness of God as that which gives and bestows. Thus for the New Testament the real sign of the righteousness of God is to be found in goodness (Rom. ii : 4 ; James i : 20). No one else but Jesus Himself has stressed emphatically that the history of God's dealings with His people and of their dealings with Him is the history of the perfect mercy and goodness of God (cf. Luke xv : 31 f.). In this above all Paul follows Him (Rom. iii : 1 ff.), and all New Testament witnesses are in Paul's company. In the New Testament, therefore, the real guilt of the Jewish people against God lies in the fact that they have not recognized the goodness of God in their history. Here, in the lack of knowledge of the nature of Divine Righteousness as God's goodness, lies then in the New Testament also the ultimate reason why the Jewish people rejected Jesus, the advocate of the goodness of God, as opposed to justice and merit (Acts iii : 17, etc.).

(iv) The new understanding of the righteousness of God as proclaimed by Jesus is made plain as the possession of His Church, not least by its attitude to the guilt of the Jewish people for the death of its Lord. The early Christian Church, on the one hand, did not at all diminish the greatness of this guilt. In fact, again and again it rigorously affirmed the guilt of the Jews for the death of Jesus as a kind of collective guilt (cf. I Thess. ii : 14 f. with Acts ii : 23 ; iii : 13 ff. ; iv : 27). But on the other hand, it left the punishment to God. Thus when the divine judgment came upon Israel the Church saw it with amazement indeed, but also with terror and not at all with complacency (cf. I Thess. ii : 16). Indeed, the Church has even regarded this judgment with sorrow and shame as a grievous distress for itself (see para. iv ; p. 30). Although religious antisemitism or anti-Judaism may have formally appealed to certain hard words of the New Testament about the Jews, in fact antisemitism even in its religious form has thoroughly misunderstood the attitude of the New Testament Church towards the ' People who murdered Christ ', and has misused its utterances to the detriment of the Church too.

(v) From the New Testament standpoint the intercourse of the Church with the Jews can be ruled only by the Law of unlimited love. The mission of the Church to Israel can be based only on the love by which the Church itself lives, and in which it seeks to share its riches with the Jews. It is not enough to base this mission on a reference to the formal missionary command, for this might oblige us to a missionary activity, but could not assure us of its spiritual justification. At the same time, we ought to be clear about the fact that missions to the Jews will be carried out on the New Testament basis only when they are carried out as unselfish service of the Church to Israel, and when they take place in the kind of relationship in which brother seeks and finds brother.

### E. PROMISE AND FULFILMENT

(i) With its election by God to be a peculiar people, Israel was placed under the Divine Promise : God would use Israel to bring salvation to all nations (Blessing of Abraham, Gen. xii : 2). The Divine Promises to Israel culminate in the promise of a Saviour King of David's race (II Sam. vii : 12, ff.). In this way the Messianic hope was founded. Later on it was manifested in a very different form. At all events we are not in a position to reconstruct it in all its details. But it can be regarded as certain that until the end of the national independence of the Jewish people it exercised a great influence. This is quite obvious from the role which it still played in the last military conflicts of the Jewish people with the Romans, under Bar Kochba.

(ii) The Messianism of Jesus certainly did not correspond with the Messianism of His people. This can be assumed, because the traditional Messianic categories—Messiah, Son of David, Moses Redivivus, perhaps even Son of Man—did not prove adequate for the Messianism of Jesus and for His understanding of His own mission. He did not recognize

Himself as destined for conquest, glory, and victory, but for service and suffering and sacrifice.

This fact, which was equally decisive for the death of Jesus and for the rise of the Church as a new congregation of election and salvation belonging to Him, gains increasing importance with reference to the Jewish people. For the Jewish people too, the traditional Messianism has more and more proved to be a blind alley. Certainly it has not completely disappeared. But just as certainly in the widest circles of Orthodox Judaism, where the messianic expectation is still cherished, the real object of the expectation today is no longer a personal Messiah, but only a state of fulfilled time and of perfect righteousness which is understood and described as messianic.

(iii) In the presence of a messianic hope, no matter how it looks in detail, even modern Judaism makes closest contact with the hope which the New Testament cherishes for the Jewish people. This hope of the Church for Israel is developed most expressly by Paul (Rom. ix–xi). But it was certainly not conceived by him, but was found by him already in the record of the words of Jesus, and simply placed by him in the great context in which it now appears (cf. already Mark xiii : 10 ; Matt. xxiv : 31, 34 ; Luke xxiii : 34 ; Matt. x : 23).

The object of this hope is that the progress of the Gospel among the nations and the winning of the nations to faith in Jesus, and their entrance into the Kingdom of God, will culminate in the entrance of all Israel into salvation. Thus the setting aside of Israel in the time of the evangelization of the nations becomes a sacrifice, and this sacrifice is offered by God's chosen people, without willing it, indeed without knowing it, for the divine purpose, that all nations should be blessed through the election of Israel. In this connection it is also expressly stated that even in this time there will not be lacking those in Israel who come to faith in Jesus and become members of His Church. But this is only spoken of in order to make plain the fact that the promise given to Israel not only has not been abolished, but is not even temporarily suspended. Rather it is fully valid for the individual Jews, and will in future remain fully valid for them. But this does not alter the fact that the Jewish people as a people are at present set aside.

(iv) The manner in which Paul, following Jesus, speaks in Romans ix–xi about Israel's destiny in the past, present, and future, nullifies any naïve optimism of the Church with respect to the evangelization of the Jews. Particularly today, when the eyes and hearts of numerous Christians are directed to the gathering of the Jews in Palestine, this cannot be emphatically enough or often enough stated.

But there is something more to be said. The manner in which Paul deals with the problem of the conversion of Israel impresses the Church with the consciousness that its opportunities have been limited by God Himself. Thus God makes plain to the Church, in the way of the Jewish people as in nothing else, that as the Church of Jesus Christ, Who is to come again and complete His work, it must not be merely a waiting Church, but an expectant Church : a Church which in the winning of the Jews to faith in Him expects Him to accomplish the last and the hardest task.

Expectation here means, however, not just complacent inactivity. Expectation means rather a waiting upon the Lord, who will call His servants to account, and so also a waiting in true service to Israel, a waiting in hope and unwearying prayer, keeping in view the whole extent of the field of work in which along with the nations Israel too is included.

This means that a Church for which the Jewish question ceases to be a question of God and its own question, and which has no room in its midst either for brotherly service to Israel or for intercession for Israel, ceases to be a Church of Jesus Christ, the Son of Abraham and the Son of David, although it may maintain an extensive and successful mission work among the Gentiles. Not the least cause of the peculiar weakness of Western Christianity in modern times may be the fact that the relationship of the Church to Israel has gone wrong, since it is at all events not what ought to be the relationship of the Church to the people chosen by God the Father of Jesus Christ.

(v) Signs are not lacking that the Jews are more aware of this state of affairs today than the Church. For the Jews today are less concerned about the message of the Church than about the Church itself, less concerned about its Word than about the witness of its life.

This is hardly a matter of chance. Rather it is rooted in the nature of Judaism as in the nature of the Church. The Church has every reason to consider what sort of question is here addressed to it ; especially as the kind of approach that Judaism is making to the Church today is very well adapted to provide decisive help and stimulus in the criticism and reform of its own self-understanding.

In particular the Church must take seriously into account the fact that the way to Jesus as the Christ for the Jews as a whole can only be through the Body of Christ (*soma christou*). It may well be that the question whether the promises given to Israel are actually fulfilled in Jesus Christ will be decided for the Jews if they can recognize in the Church, which claims to be the Body of Christ, the traits of the Messiah of the chosen people of God, Israel. At all events the way in which the Jews today are concerning themselves with the Church represents an urgent appeal to the Church, to draw all the consequences from its nature as the Body of Christ. Of course, that applies not only to the relationship with the Jews. It applies first and foremost to the relationship to its Lord Jesus Christ Himself, who according to its assurance in the Holy Spirit is the Promised One, the One who is to come, who is present in its midst, and constantly working for the coming salvation of God for all, for Jews as well as non-Jews.

III

Naturally, in a short treatment it is impossible even to indicate, far less to exhaust, all the theological problems which arise from the continued existence of the Jewish People. What this essay aims at is nothing more than a sketch of a few problems, which may suggest the importance of the whole series of problems. If it has succeeded in this, however imperfectly, the writer has reached his goal. But it would be wrong to think that a discussion of the problems is enough. And it would also be wrong to think that it would be sufficient if there were a few experts in the Church who would deal with these problems. On the contrary, the questions indicated here are such that they concern everyone who would seriously claim to be a member of the Church of Jesus Christ.

And so in closing I may express the hope that the thoughts brought forward here may help to stimulate and deepen the discussion in the Church of the Jewish question as a central question for the Church. In that event it will also be easier to bring about a more serious and deeper discussion between the Church and the Jews than any that is at present taking place or has taken place for a long time. It might be asked who would be expected to benefit most by such a discussion. Meantime I can only express my own conviction that it would be the Church. I think there are good enough grounds for this conviction.

# II

# JUDAISM TODAY

*An Evaluation of the Theological Situation of the Jewish People Today and of Contemporary Trends in Judaism*

Gösta Lindeskog

To judge a living religion from the outside is a delicate matter. Not least is this true of Judaism, with its dynamic character. To gain the requisite knowledge and understanding requires not only study of the immense, widespread body of literature, but also a penetration of Jewish spiritual life in its various phases, and an intensive personal experience of contemporary Jewish vicissitudes. Though the writer of this chapter has studied the Jewish problem and the Jewish religion for many years, he does not lay claim to that complete, all-round knowledge of the subject. Moreover, the difficulty of discussing it in some few pages will also be readily appreciated. It should therefore be pointed out that the following does not purport to be more than a description of a few aspects of an immensely rich and fascinating subject which became of interest to the writer through his studies during a recent period.

Judaism is very sensitive towards world events; its perspective is global, and it registers every disturbance and change with the vigilance of a seismograph. As always, it is centred in the world of people and in the events of history. In this respect Judaism is heir to Old Testament prophecy. This is especially true with regard to the philosophy of religion. The religious thinkers of Judaism are far from being secluded from the world. With unfailing sensibility they evaluate current history in the light of their theology. They do not live as individuals only, but as members of a people with a history and a historical consciousness such

as can be paralleled by no other people in the world.  When
a Jew to whom the concept of the Jews as a special people
is a burning reality tries from a religious angle to explain
the experiences of this generation, he sees existence as a
gigantic drama that calls for wrestling with the ancient
Jewish problem of theodicy, faith in God despite the
existence of evil—a problem he feels is more acute today
than ever.  The suffering of humanity in our generation is
intensified by, and incarnated in, the sufferings of the
Jewish people—the eternal suffering servant of the Lord.

In addition, there is another fact of boundless importance.
The foundation of the Jewish national State must, for self-
evident reasons, leave deep traces in Jewish theology.

The task with which we are concerned here is that of
catching up with Jewish thought by listening.  No great
Jewish thinker, however specialized he may be, is indifferent
to such a study.  Everywhere in Jewish literature we find
reflected the essence of Judaism.  Especially the Jewish
philosophers of religion can teach us much about religion
generally, and Judaism in particular, through their often
profound analyses of religious life and religious experience.

From early times we find in Jewish theology two ideas
about the essence of religion.  According to one of them
religion is ' rationalistic ' ;  according to the other it is
' irrationalistic '.  On the one hand it is a religion of reason ;
on the other, of revelation.  The thinkers of the Middle
Ages, Maimonides (d. 1204) and Jehuda Halevi (d. 1141),
are prototypes of these two tendencies.[1]  In addition, we
may add a third type of thinker, the type for whom religion
is *mysticism*.[2]  But an inclination toward mysticism exists
also in both the representatives of the religion of reason
and those of the religion of revelation.  Traces of these
different ideas, which we already find in the thinkers of the

[1] See Hugo Bergman, *Jewish Philosophers of Religion in Our Generation*
(Stockholm–Uppsala, 1950), p. 8 ff.  Cf. Julius Guttmann, *Die Philosophie
des Judentums* (München, 1933).
[2] A modern representative of Jewish mysticism—to mention only a
single example—was Raw Abraham Jizhak Kook (see H. Bergman,
*op. cit.*, p. 128 ff.).  Cf. G. G. Scholem, *Major Trends in Jewish Mysticism*
(1941).

Middle Ages mentioned above, confront us in different shapes in the modern Jewish philosophy of religion. This, however, is a matter upon which we cannot elaborate here.

The interpretations of the fundamental concepts of Jewish religion are extremely varied. This shows how strongly individualistic Jewish thinking on religion is, and also gives it a peculiar charm.

The old demarcations between orthodoxy, liberalism (Reform Judaism), and conservatism, which were clear and obvious until the great European catastrophe, which—rather significantly—was concentrated on the Jewish people, are still valid on the whole.[1] However, a shifting and a change are evident. The German liberalism of the nineteenth century, represented radically and persistently by such a philosopher as Hermann Cohen, hardly exists today. In a certain sense we are—to use the title of a book by Schalom Ben-Chorin—' beyond orthodoxy and liberalism '. This book seems to me to be symptomatic, though the theological programme that he puts forward there has to be considered as strictly his own on several points. This, as we already have mentioned, is highly characteristic of Jewish theology today. Jewry has at the present time important thinkers each pursuing his own separate ideas, with pronouncedly individualistic interpretations of Judaism.

There exists, of course, a standard doctrine, presented in handbooks and based on the main motives of the Old Testament and their interpretation in the literature of the Talmud and in later, more systematic condensations. It is not this ' standard theology ' that we might call the *progressive Jewish thinking in religion*. By this we mean the presentations and definitions of the independently creative, speculative philosophers of religion. It is indeed remarkable that there exists a Jewish theology which is speculative in the best sense of the word and, continually moving forward, is essentially producing, not reproducing. We are not

[1] With regard to the present division of group lines, compare *The Universal Jewish Encyclopedia*, Vol. 6, p. 238 ff., and Louis Finkelstein, ' The Jewish Religion : Its Beliefs and Practices ' (in : *The Jews : Their History, Culture, and Religion*. Ed. by L. Finkelstein. Vol II. New York, 1949), p. 1333.

4

thinking of a theology that only 'liberalizes' religion but one which, while it gathers its strength from the ancient fountains, at the same time interprets in the light of experience the fundamental Jewish ideas of religion in an individual, creative way. One could characterize Jewish theology as a living theology with a recreative power within itself.[1]

It seems to me to be characteristic of the situation that the prominent theologian Louis Finkelstein, President of the conservative Jewish Theological Seminary of America, in a presentation of 'The Jewish Religion : Its Beliefs and Practices,'[2] reprints the latest condensation by Reform Judaism of what, according to its own opinion, is basic to Judaism.[3] He provides the condensation with the following short introduction :

> In this platform no effort is made to indicate the way Reform Judaism deviates from Orthodox or Conservative interpretation of Judaism. And, indeed, the platform does not contain much to which Orthodox and Conservative groups can take exception. It is rather in its implications than by its direct statements that it deviates from tradition.[4]

It is often emphasized that dogmas do not play the same part in Judaism as in Christianity. One can even say that, on the whole, Judaism does not have dogmas in the usual sense of the word. Attempts have indeed been made on several occasions to condense the Jewish belief into a number of doctrines. A famous attempt was Maimonides' wording of the thirteen *ikkarim* (basic dogmas), which have their place in the liturgy. But it is indeed remarkable how varied,

---

[1] Compare Samuel S. Cohon : 'Neither is it (i.e. Judaism) the final revelation of God to Moses as Islam claims of Mohammed, but the progressive religious expression of the Jewish people, of its priests, prophets, sages, saints, poets, mystics, philosophers, and scholars' (*The Universal Jewish Encyclopedia*, Vol. 6, p. 235).

[2] In the compilation *The Jews : Their History, Culture, and Religion*. Edited by Louis Finkelstein. Vol. II. New York, 1949.

[3] Adopted at the meeting of the Central Conference of American Rabbis (the organization of American Reform Rabbis) in 1937. It is called after the city where the meeting took place, 'the Columbus Platform'.　　　　[4] *Op. cit.*, p. 1344.

even in rather conservative circles, are the theologians' interpretations of the belief's main substance. Nevertheless there are certain fundamental principles common to the various groups, and without which Judaism cannot be thought of.

The main block of the creed's thought is deduced from the fundamental dogma (doctrine) of Judaism : the creed of the one God, the Creator and Father, the merciful and gracious, the righteous and holy.[1] Judaism, one might say, is a creed of *Creation*. A famous passage in rabbinical literature is always quoted :

> Rabbi Akiba said : ' The words " and thou shalt love thy neighbour as thyself " constitute a great principle of the Torah.' Ben Asai said to him : ' There is a greater principle, namely, this is the Book of the Generations of Adam. In the day that God created man, in the likeness of God He created him (Gen. v : 1) '—*Sifra, Sec. Kedoshim*, Ch. iv.

In other words, from the history of Creation is deduced the belief in the value of man, the belief that all men are equal. In connection with this passage Conservative Judaism, as well as Reform Judaism, stresses that Judaism teaches an unqualified *Universalism*. Judaism is not a religion that is doing missionary work—this, also, is nowadays strongly emphasized.[2] The task of the Jewish people is to exist and to fulfil its religious task as the *people of the Covenant*.[3] Therefore there exist special rules for Jewish conduct in life, because Judaism is a *way of life*. But in addition there exists a universal ethic which corresponds to the thought of creation. This ethic must be practised not

[1] Compare Samuel S. Cohon : ' The emphasis in Judaism is not upon grace alone, but upon grace grounded in righteousness. In its vision the Divine attribute of mercy is inseparably connected with the attribute of justice.' (*The Universal Jewish Encyclopedia*, Vol. 6, p. 236.)

[2] As is known, Reform Judaism earlier willingly maintained that the task of Judaism was, through the dispersion of the Jewish people among the peoples of the world, to perform missionary work by propagation of the knowledge of the true monotheism.

[3] It is pointed out that the election is not to be considered a privilege, but a task. See, among others, Meyer Waxman, *A Handbook of Judaism as Professed and Practised through the Ages*, p. 147, and Hugo Bergman, *op. cit.*, p. 151.

only by Jews but by all peoples ; and non-Jews who fulfil
these commandments are considered as ' the righteous of
the peoples of the world '.[1]

In Judaism, *ethic* plays a primarily religious part. Judaism
teaches not an orthodoxy, but an *orthopraxy*.[2] C. G. Montefiore calls the phrase ' Through morality to religion, through
goodness to God ' the fundamental dogma of Judaism.[3]
Morals constitute the relationship between God and Man.
Salvation, atonement, personal decision, conversion, are
all ethical terms, different aspects of the ethical life.[4] The
significance of the Jewish ethic has been illustrated in innumerable descriptions in recent times. It is pointed out
that the Jewish ethic is an ethic of mind. It is denied that
the ethic is merely realistic and practical, or is a morality
of reward. Man is co-worker with God in the act of
creation : man's task, therefore, is divine, creative. In
everything, life must be a divine service ; man's task is to
be sanctified, and to sanctify life. Further it is pointed out
that Judaism has discovered the fellow-man and that the
social element is, for that reason, an integrating one in its
ethical concept.[5]

It is predominantly the Reform movement that considers
Judaism as an ethical view of life and which puts almost a
sign of equality between religion and ethics.[6] But there is
no lack of reaction against this reducing religion to an
ethical rule. We find this reaction in Schalom Ben-Chorin's
book *Jenseits von Orthodoxie und Liberalismus*. It is a basic
mistake, he says, to identify religion and ethics, a basic
mistake of which both liberalism and the new orthodoxy
are guilty. Ethics and revelation, morality and religion
are diametrically different concepts : ' Das heisst nicht,

---

[1] L. Finkelstein, *op. cit.*, p. 1334.
[2] The supposition for this distinction goes back to Moses Mendelssohn.
See H. Bergman, *op. cit.*, p. 13 ff.
[3] I. Abrahams and C. G. Montefiore, *Aspects of Judaism*, being
eighteen Sermons (2nd ed., London, 1895), p. 249.
[4] L. Pick ; *Der jüdische Idealismus* (Berlin, 1923), p. 67.
[5] The writer of this paper, in an unpublished study of Jewish theology,
has gathered quotations supporting the theses presented here.
[6] The thought that the nature of Judaism is ethics may go back to
the influence of Kant. See H. Bergman, *op. cit.*, p. 16.

dass die Religion unsittlich wäre, vielmehr ist sie *aussersittlich*. Sie steht, als Ganzes genommen, jenseits von dem, was der natürliche Mensch als gut und böse empfindet.' [1] (' That means, not that religion is unethical, but that it is supra-ethical. As a whole, it is beyond what man considers to be good and evil.')

The Jewish conception of man is optimistic. It is pointed out that man's will is free and that he possesses the power to do good. This conception of man corresponds to the doctrine of man's relationship to God. The thought of a mediator is excluded altogether, and this relates to the fact that the Jew does not know any hierarchy in, for example, the Roman Catholic sense. Rabbi and layman have an equally direct relationship with God. The doctrine of *teshuba*, conversion, has central importance. It is stressed that conversion is always open to every man and is in itself sufficient to restore the broken relationship between God and man. [2]

In my book, referred to above, I point out that Judaism can be characterized as *a-christological*. [3] That means that Judaism has been shaped in clear contrast to Christianity. What this implies is illustrated by what has been said above about the conception of man. But also in the question about the essence of faith there appears this characteristic, in contrast with Christianity. Martin Buber develops this in his book *Zwei Glaubensweisen*. There are, he says, two terms for faith. One is the Jewish term *emuna* ; the other, the Christian *pistis*. According to the first, faith is something in which one finds oneself, a way of life. It is the actual life with God : ' Israel bedeutet zuinnerst die *Unmittelbarkeit* zum unwahrnehmbaren Wesen '. [4] (' Israel in its essence signifies the immediacy of the incomprehensible Being.') This spontaneity we find in Jesus, who stands on the foundation of Judaism, but we do not find it in St Paul. There the mediator has come between. [5] *Pistis* means a logical function of the intellect : ' das Als-Wahr-annehmen

---

[1] *Op. cit.*, p. 79.
[2] In order not to dwell on this point here, I refer the reader to the discussion in my book *Die Jesusfrage im neuzeitlichen Judentum*, p. 84 f.
[3] *Op. cit.*, p. 78 ff.
[4] *Op. cit.*, p. 133.        [5] *Op. cit.*, p. 165.

und Als-Wahr-anerkennen eines verkündigten Satzes über den Gegenstand des Glaubens '.[1] (' To accept and acknowledge a doctrine of the faith.') That Buber considers to be the characteristic feature of the Christian conception of faith.

The idea of the Jews as a people is fundamental in the religion of the Old Testament. One might say that this idea is, in a way, with Israel's specific and unique faith in God, the foundation and starting-point for the Old Israelitic Jahvistic theology. It kept this dominant role until the days of reform. But in the liberal Jewish theology this idea of race underwent an essential change, losing something of its character. It was pointed out that Judaism was predominantly a religion and that it was the task of the assimilated Jews to spread the knowledge of this religion among other peoples. As a result of this reorientation, interest in the idea of the Messias and the Holy Land receded into the background. Liberal revaluation and devaluation of the nationalistic elements belonged, however, to that part of the new ideas which met with the most violent opposition, and which, in our own day, has been essentially modified by Reform Judaism itself. Characteristically, in the above-mentioned *Columbus Platform*, under the title ' Israel ' it is stated :

> Judaism is the soul of which Israel is the body . . . In the rehabilitation of Palestine, the land hallowed by memories and hopes, we behold the promise of renewed life for many of our brethren. We affirm the obligation of all Jewry to aid in its upbuilding as a Jewish homeland by endeavouring to make it not only a haven of refuge for the oppressed but also the center of Jewish culture and spiritual life.[2]

[1] *Op. cit.*, p. 176.
[2] Louis Finkelstein, *op. cit.*, p. 1345. See also Schalom Ben-Chorin, *Zionismus und Liberalismus* (Hakidmah, 30/10 1953). Compare the earlier (1885) *Pittsburgh Platform*, point 5 : 'We recognize in the modern era of universal culture of heart and intellect the approaching of the realization of Israel's great Messianic hope for the establishment of the kingdom of truth, justice, and peace among all men. We consider ourselves no longer a nation, but a religious community, and therefore expect neither a return to Palestine, nor a sacrificial worship under the sons of Aaron, nor the restoration of any of the laws concerning the Jewish state ' (Cit. David Philipson, *The Universal Jewish Encyclopedia*, Vol. 6, p. 241).

The question of the nature of Judaism, closely connected with the question of Israel as a people, belongs among the great subjects of debate, and it is fascinating to follow the settlement of this subject in Judaism itself. One to whom in large measure is due the credit of stimulating the debate upon these questions is Mordecai M. Kaplan, in, among other works, his large volume *Judaism as a Civilization: Toward a Reconstruction of American–Jewish Life* (New York, 1935). Kaplan characterizes the New-Orthodox and the Reform views of Judaism as follows :

> The Neo-Orthodox have taught that it [Judaism] is a revealed religion which so transcends all laws of social life as to be in no way affected or determined by them. As a revealed religion, Judaism is final and authoritative, destined to transform the environment but not to be transformed by it.
>
> The Reformists have interpreted Judaism as a historically evolved religion. According to them, the only bond which unites Jews is the mission to promulgate the truth about the unity of God and the brotherhood of mankind.
>
> These conceptions of Judaism have so emptied it of content that it has come to mean to most Jews nothing more than a medley of antiquated ideas and archaic practices which persists as an irrational hangover from the past.[1]

Kaplan also thinks the ' Secularists ' have in their own way contributed to obscure the true character of Judaism.

The programme which Kaplan himself develops for Jewish reorganization and renewal he summarizes under the phrase ' Judaism as a Civilization '. What that means can be explained most briefly in Kaplan's own words :

> Judaism must be recognized as nothing else than a civilization. It must figure in the consciousness of the Jew as the *tout ensemble* of all that is included in a civilization, the social framework of national unity

[1] *Op. cit.*, p. 512 f.

centering in a particular land, a continuing history, a living language and literature, religious folkways, *mores*, laws, and art ![1]

That Judaism is a civilization means that it is more than a religion. It is—perhaps one can so express Kaplan's view—the *cultural pattern* of the Jewish people, developed during thousands of years, which has its roots deep in the soul of the Jewish people, its history, and its fate. Kaplan, however, vindicates the importance of the Holy Land as a symbol for the Jewish regeneration and as a centre for Jewish civilization : ' Judaism cannot maintain its character as a civilization without a national home in Palestine '.[2] But at the same time it should be stated that according to Kaplan's conception the driving-power in Jewish civilization must be the religious element. Religion is the highest expression of civilization. Yet religion, as all other expressions of human life, is subject to the laws of development. Here, however, Kaplan wishes to make a distinction between personal religion and the religion of the people. The Jewish religion of the people exists in all the expressions of Jewish life and all forms of custom and law through which the individual identifies himself with the life and endeavours of his people. Personal religion, on the other hand, is a view of life which even the simplest Jew ought to have the freedom to develop according to his own personal convictions regarding life and the universe.[3]

Thus we have seen that the national State of Israel is considered not only as a symbol but also as a centre for Judaism, a soil from which Jewish spiritual life shall reap new harvests and give the world's Jewry new nourishment.

[1] *Op. cit.*, p. 512. Compare Samuel S. Cohon : ' Judaism, while expressed in forms and observances, which represent elements of civilization, has nevertheless functioned purely as a religion. Judaism is the spiritual way of life developed by the Jewish people ' (*The Universal Jewish Encyclopedia*, Vol 6, p. 233).

[2] *Op. cit.*, p. 516.

[3] *Op. cit.*, p. 520 f.—Through Kaplan's activity there has arisen in the U.S.A. a separate party, ' Reconstructionism '. Compare Ira Eisenstein, ' Reconstructionism ' (in : *The Universal Jewish Encyclopedia*, Vol. 6, p. 245 f.). See also Mordecai M. Kaplan : *An Evaluation*, edited by Ira Eisenstein and Eugene Kohn (New York, 1952).

*Mutatis mutandis*, the old word of the Prophet has acquired renewed actuality :

> For out of Zion shall go forth the Law,
> and the word of the Lord from Jerusalem.
> (Isaiah ii : 3)

The idea is fascinating and, for the Jewish religious thinking of our time, must be a source of inspiration of extreme importance with regard to new, creative enterprises. It meets resistance as usual, however, when it encounters the firm, recalcitrant matter of reality. As the Christian, so also the Jewish population of the world has experienced during decades a thorough-going process of secularization. Hugo S. Bergman, in a series of lectures on the modern Jewish philosophy of religion delivered at Stockholm during the winter of 1947–48, discussed that problem, among others.[1] One has tried, says Bergman, to keep a part of the Jewish inheritance, for example, the idea of the land of promise. Secularized Zionism changed, by its secularization, a profound religious idea into a nationalistic myth.[2] Bergman readily admits that Zionism has been an important factor in counteracting elements that would destroy the identity of the Jewish people ; but it is his conviction that a secularized Zionism cannot save Judaism.[3] A passage by the same author which appears in a volume commemorating the twenty-fifth anniversary of the founding of the Hebrew University of Jerusalem is of great interest. There it is stated :

> We have rejected the ideology of missionary Judaism, which counted the dispersion of the Jewish people as a blessing. A noble exponent of the idea of missionary Judaism, the philosopher Oscar Ewald, said : ' The dispersion of the Jewish people throughout the world has a human significance from the point of view of world history, and not merely the character of a transient exile. Scattered Jewry is the seed of united humanity in the future.' We rejected that idea because we

---

[1] Published in Swedish under the title *Judiska religionsfilosofer i vår generation* (Stockholm–Uppsala, 1950),which book has been quoted above.
[2] *Op. cit.*, p. 150.　　　　　[3] *Op. cit.*, p. 16.

believed that Judaism would be fulfilled not by preaching and propaganda, but through the actual building
of a Jewish society in the land of Israel.  But, just as
we rejected that pale ideology, so too we must reject
the idea that in the land of Israel there should come
into being a purely secular people like all other nations,
which refuses to take cognisance of the religious and
spiritual past of the Jewish people.  And there are
many alarming symptoms that developments in Israel
are taking that course.[1]

It is certainly a 'great task'.  Much depends on how
this task is to be carried out.  With excitement one is
waiting to see how the religious life in Israel will develop.
Perhaps there will grow up, on its own national soil, a new
philosophy of religion which may become a powerful
factor in the spiritual life of world Jewry.

With these words, we stand on the threshold of the future,
and so another aspect of Jewish religion must be considered,
which always has been characteristic of it, its Futurism.  In
Christian exegetics of the present time there is a diversity
of opinion as to what this concern for the future meant at
the time of the Old Testament.  Some maintain that
Messianism is an ancient conception in the religion of
Israel ;  others, that 'Messias' in its proper sense is a
relatively late conception, dating from the time after the
exile.  According to some, Jewish eschatology was firmly
developed at the time of the early prophets ;  according to
others, it appears, in its proper sense, first in the Apocalyptics.
It is a fact, however, that belief in a Messianic age has at
all times been an integral part of Judaism.[2]  This vital
conception also became subjected by Reform Judaism to
an at times rather radical revaluation.  But futurism is
still a well-preserved part of the edifice of the Jewish
theological system.  Here we shall not deal with the
traditional hope for the Messias in Orthodox Judaism but

[1] 'A Great Task' (*The Hebrew University of Jerusalem* 1925–1950,
p. 173 f.).  See also Schalom Ben-Chorin, *Zur religiösen Lage in Palästina*
(Tel-Aviv, 1940).
[2] Compare Meyer Waxman, *A Handbook of Judaism as Professed and
Practised Through the Ages* (New York, 1947) p. 159 ff.

centre our attention upon some aspects that appear in the
futurism of progressive Judaism and that might be of
interest in this connection.

We have mentioned earlier that Jewish thinking is
*optimistic*. This optimism is reflected also, and not least, in
the view of the future. There we find also the Jewish
*universalism*. Both these features are most clearly evident in
the futurism of Reform Judaism. To quote again from the
*Columbus Platform* :

> We regard it as our historic task to co-operate with all
> men in the establishment of the Kingdom of God, of
> universal brotherhood, justice, truth and peace on
> earth. This is our Messianic goal.[1]

The Kingdom of God . . . on earth—thus can the
Jewish ' eschatology ' be most succinctly expressed and this,
again, demonstrates a contrast to Christian theology. Louis
Finkelstein tries to sum up as follows a consensus of opinion
among modern Jews on these questions :

> Reform and many Conservative Jews expect that the
> Messianic age will come about through the gradual
> enlightenment of men and through the work of many
> thinkers and teachers. All agree that the age will be
> one of profound and universal faith in God, recognition
> of human brotherhood, and an unprecedented know-
> ledge of the universe.[2]

In respect to its view of the future, modern Judaism
stands on the ground of the Old Testament. The Kingdom
of God is a men's kingdom of peace on earth—in contrast
to the late-Jewish theory of catastrophe in the Apocalypse,
which did not count on any earthly progress but implied
the belief in the destruction of the old world and in a new,
cosmic creation : ' New heavens and a new earth '—a
thought that appears sporadically in the later parts of the
Old Testament (Isa. lxv : 17).[3] It is entirely natural that
the Holy Land should play a central role in the perspective

---

[1] Louis Finkelstein, *op. cit.*, p. 1345.
[2] *Op. cit.*, p. 1342.
[3] Compare Schalom Ben-Chorin, *op. cit.*, p. 121 ff.

of the future.[1] Now that the country has become a ' realized eschatology ', there begins for Judaism a new phase of history, from a new religious date ; but it remains to be seen what consequences for the Jewish view of the world and of life the confrontation of idea and reality—the reality of everyday life in Israel—will have. Will the idea have power sufficient to form the future of the Jewish people ? This it should have.

It is of vital interest for Christian theology that it follow attentively the Jewish philosophy of religion and Bible research. Here a scheme appears which, in its monumentally simple lines, allows us to come close to the nature of Judaism and gives us an important standard with which to evaluate the unique quality of Christianity ; for in Judaism we learn to know a religion that has arisen from the same assumptions as Christianity, but has developed a basic religious conception differing in vital respects from Christianity. To keep abreast of developments in Jewish theology, however, is an extensive task that requires specialists and, preferably, special professorships at Christian universities. In order to get an idea of the import of the task it is enough to remind ourselves of the literature of Israel in Hebrew which, now in its beginnings, shows promise of a splendid development.

In my book *Die Jesusfrage im neuzeitlichen Judentum* I tried to give an account of Jewish theology's way of dealing with the central problems of Christianity. This discussion about the question of Christ, about the origin of Christianity and Christian dogmatics, continues. It is surprising to observe how carefully Jewish scholars follow Christian literature on these questions. As I see it now, a renewed, profound study on our part is necessary in order to bring our understanding of the Jewish investigations up to date : a study aiming at a confrontation of the Christian and Jewish interpretations of the Bible, of the Old as well as of the New Testament. A major problem is the question of Paul and the related one about the suppositions for the Pauline settlement with Judaism. These problems must be re-examined in Christian exegetics, with serious consideration given to their treatment

[1] Compare Ben-Chorin, *op. cit.*, p. 122.

by Jewish scholars. In this connection I think especially of Joseph Klausner's large work *From Jesus to Paul*, and Martin Buber's earlier-mentioned *Zwei Glaubensweisen*. Already the latter offers a not insignificant field for research. It is rich in ideas and reinterpretations which require testing. That which makes the study of such a book an important task is the penetration into the depths of religious phenomena that is so characteristic of its author.

Through my many years of study of the subject I have had reason to ask myself whether one could not soon expect a new phase in this part of Jewish religious study, a phase characterized by settlement with the newest currents in Christian exegetics. I believe I can say that certain signs do point in this direction. Such are to be found, it seems to me, in, for example, some recent publications of Professor Hans Joachim Schoeps, viz. *Aus frühchristlicher Zeit: Religionsgeschichtliche Untersuchungen* (Tübingen, 1950) and *Gottheit und Menschheit: Die grossen Religionsstifter und ihre Lehren* (Stuttgart, 1950). I shall call attention here only briefly to Schoeps' way of describing Jesus and early Christianity. He is convinced that eschatology played a central role in the gospel of Christ ; that Jesus was aware of being the Messias ; and that the foundation of the Church rests upon two facts—faith in the resurrection, and the institution of the Lord's Supper. It is incomprehensible, states Schoeps, that liberal theology could at any time doubt the Messianic awareness of Jesus. But he thinks there already existed an enhancement in the Christology of early Christianity in comparison with Jesus' own self-consciousness : very early the Messias-Son of Man became the Christ-Son of God of the Christian faith. In themselves, these ideas are not entirely new in the Jewish study of Jesus. But it seems to me that Schoeps, taking into account the latest Christian studies, has tried to reach a more objective religious-historical judgment on the question concerning the origins of Christianity than has been held earlier. Intention and wording are new, in part, as is also the direction of interest.

Jewish research has made particularly important contributions in various fields of exegetics of the New Testament.

It is obvious, also, that acquaintance with Jewish studies in
this field can have a quite practical interest, *viz.* for the discussion of religion between the Synagogue and the Church
—a discussion in which Schoeps himself, among others, has
vigorously engaged.[1]

In its more radical manifestations Reform Judaism signified a profound change for Judaism. As every other
phenomenon in the history of spiritual life, it developed
under the inherent laws of evolution. Reaction did not fail
to appear, and this reaction, as is clear from what has been
said above, has in turn left its mark on the Reform movement itself. If, in closing, one should attempt to characterize
summarily the present situation, it could be said that Judaism
is now in a stage of *consolidation*, despite great uncertainty
and dissension in the religious field.[2] The organic unity of
the Jewish religion with the people is again stressed with
increasing strength. The connection with the past also is
vindicated by the advocates of evolution. The revival of
the Hebrew language is a powerful factor in modern Jewish
spiritual life. The evolving of an Israelitic national culture
is an inspiration to every Jew who feels as a Jew. In spite
of the acute physical suffering among the Jewry of Central
Europe at present, and in spite of the inconceivable spiritual
martyrdom of these times, the people's body is healthy and
strong. The Jewish people has found its way home to its
own land. It may, also, find its way home in a spiritual
sense.

---

[1] See his book *Jüdisch-Christliches Religionsgespräch in neunzehn Jahr-
hunderten: Die Geschichte einer theologischen Auseinandersetzung* (Frankfurt
a.M., 1949).
[2] In the U.S.A. a spiritual-religious revival seems to have appeared
in the ranks of its Jewry. A symptom of that appears in a book by
Will Herberg, *Judaism and Modern Man: An Interpretation of Jewish
Religion* (New York). In that book are expressions which remind one
of Søren Kierkegaard and Karl Barth. Herberg considers history as
a tragedy: it is the history of fallen man. The solution cannot be
found in an immanent progress of human life, but in a transformation
of it through a transcendent, divine intervention. This interpretation
of history, however, stands in absolute contrast to that of Jewish
liberalism. Of this book Hugo Bergman has written a critical review
(in: *Judisk Tidskrift*, 1953, pp. 17–21, Stockholm) which illustrates in
an interesting way the opposing tendencies in present-day Jewish
religion.

# FAITH AND THE JEWISH LAW TODAY

Hans Joachim Schoeps

We Jews of the mid-twentieth century live today in what may be called, without exaggeration, a post-Jewish situation. That is to say, the reality of each day's living is such that it is no longer possible for most of us to experience our Jewishness immediately and at any moment. This is true for both America and Europe—it may even apply to the secular State of Israel—and must be fully appreciated by anyone who hopes to say something about the present situation of Judaism that is to the point.

It is time for us to renounce all fictions of the ' as if ' kind. We cannot act as if we were still living in the ghetto and as if it were possible artificially to keep alive the ways of life that flourished there ; we cannot act as if the laws of the Torah still signified for us the rules of conduct ; as if fear of God and not self-aggrandizement were the common fact ; as if the sermon's conventional opening words, ' Worshipful congregation ', really applied to those seated beneath the pulpit, who may be ready to listen to their rabbi's opinions only if he is a ' good speaker '. There is no point in deceiving ourselves : the Jew of today may be the grandson or great-grandson of a pious man, but he himself is completely a man of his age. The newspaper has more interest for him than the Bible, and he prefers the cinema to an edifying midrashic (not to say halachic) discourse.

And, really, there is a question as to whether he is not perhaps right, after all, in his preference ; for the events enacted on the film screen probably have more meaning for him in the concrete circumstances of his life than an exposition of a problem in the Law or in the ritual regulations of cleanliness. Law and ritual are often something he no longer even understands, or at least can no longer regard as meaningful and apposite to the problems of his daily living. It is of little help to the Jew of today to ponder the problems his fathers racked their brains about, for the circumstances out of which the problems sprang have disappeared or grown incomprehensible. What a friend of mine wrote in connection with the Maimonides memorial year (1935) has a general validity : ' On the whole it is impossible to make an alien existence one's own ; the best one can do is . . . to co-exist with it. But there are already great stretches of time for which this is no longer possible. The eight hundred years that separate the Jews of today from Maimonides are not to be rolled back. There is only the hope that—if we genuinely enquire in our time as to the meaning of Judaism—we shall somewhere, sometime, light upon Maimonides. . . . True studying, however, means first of all not Maimonides, it means ourselves.'

The question, then is : how shall a modern man reconcile the Judaism that was with the Jew that he is ?

As the Jews of all previous centuries understood it, the great turning-point in Jewish history, the first real breach of the historical tradition, was the destruction of the Temple by the Romans under Titus in the year 70 C.E. It is generally agreed that we have the Pharisaic theologians of the time to thank for the fact that this rupture of the historical tradition did not prove fatal and put an end to Jewish history altogether. It was the sages of Jabneh, of Lydda, of Caesarea, and Bene-Brak, who were the first to develop the concept of the ' as if ' into an enduring principle of Jewish history. The Theocracy no longer existed, but its constitution remained in force as if it did. The Temple no longer existed, but Jews the world over bowed in prayer in its direction as if it did. The High Priest no longer made his expiatory sacrifice on the Day of Atonement, but the ritual formula was learned and recited on that day as if he did. Meanwhile, other things took the place of the actual sacrifice : study of Torah, good works, prayer—the fulfilling of these commandments counted as much as the animal sacrifice of ancient times.

This disregard of the actual facts, this abstracting of Judaism from every reality of the here and now, was a phenomenal accomplishment. It did indeed ' save ' Judaism —that is to say, by means of the ' as if ', Judaism was adapted to exile and was removed to the plane of the timeless. The faith of the Jews proved more real than reality and overcame it. The sages of Jabneh assumed, as the most self-evident thing in the world, that the royal decrees of God the King as set forth in the constitution of the Covenant (the Torah) were as valid in their day as before. Hence they strove, by putting up ' a fence around the Torah ', to preserve Judaism in isolation from time and space. From Johanan ben Zakkai to Joseph Caro, law was heaped on law, and in defiance of all reasonable expectation Judaism was successfully translated to the plane of the timeless, the Jews learning to live their lives more or less alongside of time.

This was a greater feat than Alexander's conquests or the empire of the Caesars. For it effected a paradoxical retroactive annulment of historical fact : the Jewish state turned out not to have fallen at all in the year 70, but was preserved in its laws and lived on, metamorphosed, in the ghetto. It was Johanan ben Zakkai, the betrayer of his country to the Romans, who became its saviour, and not the nationalist Bar Kochba, whose reaction to his country's disgrace was only—a patriot's. The sages of Jabneh proved more far-sighted than the Zealots, with a far-sightedness that reached seventeen hundred years into the future. During this time they reigned supreme—because the laws they had clung to did not remain mere fictions but *became a reality through faith*. It was only in an age of disbelief that they became fictions—that is, about the beginning of the period of Western European emancipation.

It is therefore this emancipation that is the most fateful breach in the continuity of Jewish history, for this time there was no bridge improvised to span the abyss. Where the Tannaim of the second century had succeeded in making over the Law to suit the new historical epoch, the Reform rabbis of the nineteenth century signally failed. Now the

5

thread was really broken, and the great question that had lain hidden all these years, in the heart of the year 70, first revealed itself for what it really was : the question of Judaism's destiny.  The emancipation for the first time shattered the inner historical coherence of Judaism and put an end to the legislative power of the Jewish state, which thanks to Johanan ben Zakkai had maintained a fictitious existence through faith seventeen hundred years beyond its actual end.  With the disappearance of the ghetto, faith as a collective phenomenon and the all-inclusive regulation of life according to the Mosaic Law ceased to exist.

Moses Mendelssohn's generation was the last to hold completely with the sages of Jabneh, regulating their lives according to the unabridged Mosaic Law as fixed by Moses Isserles and Joseph Caro.  Since then the number of families remaining faithful to the Law—of whom Samson Raphael Hirsch was a representative spokesman in the nineteenth century—has steadily declined.  For a host of others, whose numbers increased generation after generation as the observance of the Law fell off (until only a pure distillation of the ethical element—little more than the Ten Commandments—remained), the ancient Law was but a fiction, because faith was lacking.

Once the fence was torn down, and once the Jews had established themselves in the new reality of the modern world, all further need of the ' as if ' became superfluous. However, from Michael Creizenach and S. L. Steinheim to Leo Baeck, Jewish thinkers have been sensible of the void that has arisen within, and now began to pose more and more urgently the question of the ' essence of Judaism '. Their question, in short, was : what now was left of Judaism ?

What is it, in a Law suffering a gradual loss of all authority, that is worthy of surviving ?  What is the Jewish faith today ?  Wherein is it to be found and how can it be established ?

There is nothing in the Jewish tradition to countenance the asking of such questions ; and because such questions were never asked before, no earlier answers exist to guide us today. All those who have not perceived the belated manifestation, commencing about 1800, of the fatality concealed in the year 70, who have not perceived the growing untenability of the ' as if ' set down by the sages of Jabneh, will never recognize the right to ask these questions. But it is vital for us that we ask them, for it has ceased to be apparent why the body of the Jewish people should still maintain its separate identity if the individual Jew is going to know as little as he does about the origin (election) and end (God's supremacy) of the Covenant, and its constitutional obligations (Law).

It is therefore legitimate to ask what are the basic tenets of the Jewish faith—on this question the further existence of Judaism depends. If one has a deep enough understanding of the question, deeper at any rate than the nineteenth century's, one must ask oneself if it is possible for men today to realize the Covenant in their lives. The man of today, no longer feeling any need to justify himself before God, answerable only to himself for his observance or non-observance of the Law, will no longer countenance God, faith, Law, and the Covenant of Israel as the *a priori* of his consciousness or the whole content of his life. Jewish Orthodoxy has nothing to say to him. For it to speak to modern man, it would have to be able to divorce itself from its presuppositions, and its very inability to do so is what constitutes its greatness ; if it could really make itself comprehensible to him, it would cease being Jewish Orthodoxy. The Levitical laws of purification, or the concept underlying the application of most of Jewish Law—that man, by the correct fulfilment of these laws, from time to time becomes *yotseh* (perfect) before God—are now as incomprehensible as the well-reasoned *halachic* belief that the turning on of an electric light or talking on the telephone on the Sabbath is against the will of God. The direct and unbroken connection of civilized life in the twentieth century with the will of God manifested four thousand years ago can no longer be perceived.

The *factum brutum* confronting us today is just this apparently ineradicable disharmony which has arisen between life under the Law and the modern secular scientific and technological understanding of reality.

Yet to almost every living Jew for whom the Bible is not an entirely closed book, the answer to God's summonses that men once made with their lives can never be lost. Even in periods most distant from the primal source, these constitutive events of Judaism will be understood, and Jews must willy-nilly hear the words by which Scripture has declared their eternal election and preservation. For Jewishness—which connotes not merely the experience of antisemitism but also the sense of an eternal pattern and recurrence—is an ineluctable destiny, as we in the mid-twentieth century are coming to recognize. Events have prompted us once again to discover ourselves as Jews. It is no longer the case today that the Jewish teachings instruct us in our destiny, but rather that our Jewish destiny recalls us to the forgotten Jewish teachings. Thus our way to Judaism lies in a direction clean contrary to tradition's : our way is that of a modern, historically conscious Jewish theology.

If a modern Jew who has blithely accepted the life he leads as a citizen of contemporary America or Europe or the State of Israel comes to question the meaning of his Jewish origin, which even in the twentieth century causes him to suffer the fate of the Jew, then Jewish theology has a real answer to give to this question. The answer goes something like this : our sufferings have their origin in the denial or forgetting of something that goes back three and a half millennia and which has nothing at all to do with our being ' for ' or ' against ' it—an event that befell our fathers, was reported in the Bible, and so has been handed down through all history. God elected Israel to receive His Covenant, out of His free will He chose one people among the many on the earth. To understand the essence and the destiny of the Jewish people, one must understand its origin as being spiritual yet real : God took one people for His own, calling it to represent His royal will : ' Ye shall be Mine own treasure from among all peoples ; for all the earth is Mine ; and ye shall be unto Me a kingdom of priests, and a holy nation ' (Ex. xix : 5–6). Or as Buber has translated it, giving a sharper accent to its meaning : ' And ye shall become unto Me a realm of priests, a nation singled out from amongst all the others.' Israel, by the unfathomable will of God, was chosen as the object of His intention to conclude a compact with His creation. The terms of this pact, ever since the event on Sinai, are the Law of the Torah, by which the Jews shall be placed under God's will. Taken, therefore, in the legitimate Jewish sense, the Covenant is an objective matter that has nothing to do with the will, wish, or allegiance of the individual Jew, and thus is not dependent on whether a modern Jew can comprehend it or not. At Moriah, and in the promise made to Abraham, all the seed of Israel were chosen—everyone born of a Jewish mother since that time has a share in Abraham's election, becomes with Isaac a son of the promise, and by his birth acquires membership in the Covenant. The external symbol of this is circumcision, marking the Jew as a sharer in the Covenant of Abraham. This is circumcision's ' sacramental ' meaning—it is not a hygienic measure, but a means by which to annihilate the historical distance dividing the Jewish child from the primal father Abraham ; through circumcision a Jewish child becomes contemporaneous with Abraham.

Today we see how this sacrament has lost its efficacy, how it is no longer possible to achieve this contemporaneity, because our being, as determined for us by Jewish destiny, and our consciousness, as modern men, gape apart. This schism of being and consciousness is the crisis in which we find ourselves today. The modern-minded Jew no longer acknowledges his original Jewish destiny, abandons that law of his origins which separated him from the world, and tries to dwell in the world as a man like other men. But the destiny of his being, that being which his membership in the Jewish collectivity willy-nilly gives him, does not change because his consciousness has changed ; the schism between the two is the Jewish fate as we know it today. There is no variety of assimilation that permanently succeeds, neither the assimilation of individuals nor that other assimilation which in the name of modern nationalism would like to place the Jewish nation under laws derived from other nations. It has never failed to eventuate, in all the centuries that lie behind us, that an Israel wanting to flee from itself, to throw off the yoke of its separateness, has been compelled to resume its life apart, its ' sanctification '. ' And they shall be upon thee for a sign and for a wonder, and upon thy seed for ever. The Lord shall scatter thee among all peoples, from the one end of the earth even unto the other end of the earth. And among these nations shalt thou find no ease, and there shall be no rest for the sole of thy foot ; but the Lord shall give thee there a trembling heart, and failing of eyes, and pining of soul ' (Deut. xxviii : 46, 64–65).

Now these are all things that a modern man with faith can very well see for himself ; for they are part of a history that continually repeats itself, and which those generations, in particular, upon whom the punishment is visited learn to understand. In every case this is what we are left with : the responsibility of reflecting on the underlying causes of our Jewish destiny in order to arrive at a true understanding of it. This indeed is not yet Jewish faith, but taking thought in this way may lead to it. By this historical-theological approach, by coming to know the continuity of Jewish history, we catch sight of a part of the Jewish reality that otherwise would be concealed from us. It can, indeed, inspire a man with a truer adherence to the Jewish reality than all the so-called ' positive ' approaches, which in the last analysis are for the most part merely unreal and anachronistic attempts artificially to reconstruct the past.

The historical-theological approach by itself can do no more than teach the modern Jew a historical lesson ; it cannot make a believer out of him, change the reader of a ' sacred hieroglyph ' (Ranke) into one who beholds the revelation of the living God. It can only lead him to the threshold, confront him with the Jewish reality ; all the learned study in the world cannot do more than this. To go farther—for the person who has been led to acknowledge

the spiritual truths of Jewish history, to become a believer—
he must turn from the general and abstract to the personal
and concrete ; the historical truth of the election of Israel
that he has perceived must pass out of his abstract understanding and be realized in his personal existence. And
this brings us to the last possibility of contemporary man.
The laws recorded in the Bible must be felt not only as
commandments to the generation of the wilderness, but to
oneself : God's word spoken to oneself to which one makes
answer with one's life. How this happens it is impossible
to say, because it is one of the secrets between God and man.
One can and must, however, speak of what it leads to ;
for everything leading to the reality of the Covenant leads
to the charter of this Covenant—the Law.

When a modern Jew thinks of the Law, it is of a series of
' fine old customs ' whose practice was an important part
of the life of his parents or grandparents. A Jewish theology
that simply insisted that these ' fine old customs ' are the
' real ' Judaism he is seeking would be a deception. It is
of course possible in every age to experience God's will in
forms and customs too ; yet one must first have felt it at
a deeper level of one's being.

A man who has grown aware of Judaism's importance
to him is not helped appreciably by a theology that sends
him to the ritual precepts of the book of Leviticus without
at the same time telling him that he will understand their
meaning only after he has read the books of Genesis and
Exodus. He will not then, as he reads, pass lightly over
the account, at the beginning of the Bible, of Adam's disobedience to God. He will not fail to see the exemplary
character of this first man's disobedience (sin), endlessly
repeated in the lives of all the sons of Adam (particularly
of the great ones of this earth). God, however, it is shown
to him, keeps faith with the faithless, and in mercy makes
his Covenant with one people whom he has called from
among the peoples of mankind. This Covenant is based
upon the promise and the Law. The Law points out to
each man, and each generation, who are forever back-
sliding anew, the right path to what is ' good ' in the eyes

of God. The generation that was vouchsafed the revelation, the generation of the wanderings in the wilderness, handed down as Law what for them had been their answer to the divine summons. However, each subsequent generation faces the task of distinguishing, amid the precepts and prohibitions recorded for the most part in Leviticus, God's commandment to it—that is, through the Law it must come to understand the revelation.

Martin Buber once wrote as follows to Franz Rosenzweig on this point : ' I don't believe that revelation is ever lawgiving ; and in the fact that lawgiving is always its result I see the fact of human contradiction, the human factor.' God's pure word is changed in Moses' mouth into human words and dogma, God's pronouncement veils itself in the Law of Torah, the Word vanishes behind the word. But this insight of Buber's does not lead to a flat rejection of Law. He does not doubt that the generation receiving the revelation truly perceived the will of God ; there is only the doubt that God's will as handed down—the Law as fixed in the Torah—can be taken over wholesale in later times by generations not vouchsafed the revelation. To make it truly one's own life, as Buber puts it, ' only so much of it [the Law] must be acknowledged as I can acknowledge as having been said to me '. In this way, to be sure, the universal validity of the Law is lost ; but this loss of the unchanging and universal Law is precisely what defines the modern situation.

Despite this loss of a universal and timeless valid Law, I believe certain things can be asserted with confidence. The first and foremost religious possibility for the individual is and will always be through the ethical. Though in the Bible the moral commandments go hand in hand with the ritual, sacrificial, dietary, and marriage laws, they are nevertheless separable from them. Tradition was well aware of this, but had no reason to attribute any great importance to the matter. Today, however, the pre-eminence of the ethical is plain, for the moral law is an elementary demand whose insistence every human being can feel (hence the primacy of the Decalogue for all men), whereas

this is not at all the case with the dietary laws or the sacrificial regulations.

Thus, for example, the force of the commandment
' Thou shalt love thy neighbour as thyself ' can be felt by
everyone in every age for the very reason that man does
not love his neighbour, does not keep his neighbour's good
in mind.   But there it can happen that one feels one's
offence, and in the distress of this feeling can come to see
one's behaviour for what it is, a falling away from the will
of God.   In the moment that a man acknowledges his guilt
the word of God has found its way to him.   In discovering
that God's will and man's wish are not the same, the primal
wound of life is opened in him, and he is driven by the pain
he feels to seek that help which human hands can no longer
give him.   In this divergence of the human and the divine,
God's sovereign claim upon mankind is recognized and
man's faith in his supposed self-sufficiency dwindles to
nothing.   For in the claim that God asserts upon us by
His commandments we feel our helplessness, we realize
that everything we are and have is held in fee from Him, is
a sign of the creature whom his Creator has summoned to
do His will.   Where this original disparity between the
Almighty God and creature man is made to live again,
there is always the possibility of God's drawing near to us
out of His remoteness, His will coming to guide our life,
His commandment passing into our life as ' Law '.

Life is not a pursuing of necessarily brief and infrequent
encounters with the Divine, but a continual living and doing
of what in these encounters we have been called upon by
the Divine to do—a living of the Law.   Yet it is also true
that the Torah can never become the law of man's life
today without his discovering it for himself in this encounter
with the Divine ;  for modern scepticism forbids his accepting
his forefathers' laws unless he has learned their validity
through his own experience.   Today the realization of the
Law is only possible to a post-sceptical attitude of faith that
has itself weathered every doubt.

At this point, to be sure, a host of questions confront us.
How many and which of the laws is it possible to realize

today ?  Will it be possible eventually to realize all the Torah laws, or is it not the very nature of this modern religious attitude to bar us from realizing the majority of them ?  At what point will a halt be called, or will the modern man of the Torah go on to make the law of the red cow a constituent part of his life ?  What implications are there in this approach for adult religious education ?

Merely to ask these questions, however, shows how impossible it is to fix a new objective standard of the law. No new Shulchan Aruch can be truly derived from the modern sentiment—to try to do so, as many Reform and Conservative Jews would like, would merely bring on a schism.  The way of all those who, in our time, have seen the star of the Covenant and have gone forth to make the Law once again an effective reality in their lives, lies through the same old countryside but no longer along the same road. For, Franz Rosenzweig once wrote, ' there has been no road there these one hundred and fifty years.  Its prolongation into modern times, to be sure, " is still there ", but under the best of circumstances this is only one among innumerable roads, no longer *the* road.  So we shall have to content ourselves with the unity of the countryside.  Let us hope that the day will come when there will be a main road running through it once again.  And I believe that that day will come.  Or rather not some one road surely, but a system of roads perhaps.  But this can only be guesswork today. It isn't time yet for systems.  Building our individual roads, however, is the right way to go about it.'

Franz Rosenzweig himself found such a way, a way to recapture and reintegrate Jewish Law with one's personal life ; he returned to the observance of *kashrut*, to respect for the Sabbath, and to daily prayers.  He achieved all this step by step, and by himself.  He championed ' something ', *his* ' something ', against Orthodox Jews who wanted ' everything ' and atheist Jews who wanted ' nothing '.  In a letter to Rudolf Hallo, dated November 27, 1922, he wrote :

Here, as everywhere else, I reject this Everything-or-Nothing politics.  Neither the Everything nor the

Nothing belongs to us ; the Something does. The Something is given to us. We have to settle ourselves down in the Something. I don't say that my particular Something is an example for anyone else. What may be taken as an example is that I have the courage—just as much against the idealists of the Nothing as against those of the Everything—to live in my Something. This cannot be exemplary as regards detail. I'm really only beginning. I don't know what will come out of it, and don't want to know. I hope and know that others are beginning, too. Something exemplary will develop out of the whole. I, we, all those who don't say ' Everything or Nothing ' are today trying once more to do what Jewish liberalism tried to do a hundred years ago and failed in. It failed because it tried to set up principles first and then act according to them. These principles remained, like the ones they opposed, officers without soldiers, hence fathers without children. We begin with the act. Let the principle for it be formed in time to come, by ourselves or by others. I silently hope that, some day, in decades, I shall know the principles, the laws, ' the Law ', at last, and that I shall once again be able to open my mouth and teach. But it doesn't matter, whether it's I or others—the best would be : I and others.

A deep insight into the nature of the Law is at the bottom of this. Judaism is not Law. It creates Law, but is not Law itself. It ' is ' being a Jew.

What Rosenzweig again and again came back to was living experience, not the dead appropriation of stores of knowledge, forms of tradition, or even the imitation of Biblical Law in one's own life out of inner necessity. The Law, which as written in the Bible stands for everyone, should in this hour become a living command precisely for me. And anyone who studies Torah in the right frame of mind can, like me, come upon this retransformation of Law into commandment. Rosenzweig experienced what had been experienced in ages past : the priority of revelation over Law, the priority of God as lord over God as lawgiver. ' Only man in his sluggishness changes the commands into Law—by the way in which he carries them out—

changes them into something systematized, capable of being obeyed without fear and trembling.'

Franz Rosenzweig's way has been an example for many people of our era ; but neither his way nor another's can serve us all in common. All of us today must go our several ways—ultimately, we feel sure, to arrive at the one goal where all our ways shall meet. That goal lies beyond all our individual lives. We have no authoritative Judaism of our own to set over against that of earlier times or against the Judaism of those among us who still represent that earlier time in their lives, and we may look ashamed on all our miserable efforts bespeaking, it would seem, no more than the weakness of our faith. Yet such as it is, we must stand by it as our life's reality, and seek to realize so much of the Torah as we individually can, according to our living faith. We may feel ashamed and self-conscious at setting aside Friday evenings for quiet conversation with friends, instead of going to the Synagogue and lighting candles at home. But if that is all we can—that is what we must do.

So long as every one of us today strives to make real the possibility that is his, we can be certain that our contemporary Jewish faith, for all its inability to realize the Law in full, has not yet ceased to be part of the tradition.

And should we meet, as we go our way, with those figures standing at the beginning of post-Biblical history, I am confident that the great rabbis will indeed smile in astonishment at the appearance of their descendants, but they will surely never despise us. They, who have handed down sayings that all our ponderings shall never exhaust, will surely stand in awe before the mystery of God's ways. Ben Azzai said : ' Despise no man and deem nothing impossible ; for there is not a man that has not his hour, and there is not a thing that has not its place ' (Aboth, iv : 3).

# IV

# THE EMERGENCE OF THE STATE OF ISRAEL AND ITS SIGNIFICANCE FOR THE CHRISTIAN CHURCH

### R. Clephane Macanna

THERE is an element of inevitability in the emergence of the State of Israel in the year 1948. During their long dispersion the Jews have remained a people apart. Scattered throughout the whole world they have maintained their identity. Although without a homeland, and although persecution and assimilation have from time to time reduced their numbers, they have survived. This sense of being a separate people was based on their religion, and that religion was tied firmly to their past in Palestine. Their whole tradition was bound to Jerusalem and to the land of which it was the capital. Jews who thought of themselves as citizens of the countries in which they lived, differing from their fellows only in the matter of religion, were a very small group, and it is only over the last hundred years that this viewpoint has emerged. The great majority have always accepted the fact of their difference from their fellow-citizens, and persecution and antisemitism have driven this point home. For the vast majority of Jews there has been little opportunity to lose their identity, or their memories of the Promised Land, by absorption. Attempts there have been to find a territory where a new Jewish State could be rebuilt, but these have foundered for a variety of reasons. Not the least of these reasons has been the memory of Jerusalem.

The inauguration of the Jewish National Home in Palestine after the first World War was an attempt to meet a need of the Jews, but there never was any thought of such a National Home being established to the detriment of the population of Palestine at that time. The failure of the experiment was certainly due to factors which did not exist when the planners of the National Home formulated their scheme. World opinion regarding the idea was neither cordial nor violently opposed, and the general indifference was even shared by world Jewry. The number of Jews emigrating to Palestine in the first ten years after World War I was small. It was the desperate situation for Jews in Europe, which began with Hitler's coming to power in Germany, that set the flood of Jewish emigration towards Palestine. Unfortunately this sudden increase in the number of Jews roused the fears of the Arab population and whipped up a frenzy of Arab nationalism. Earlier doubts regarding the National Home had been allayed by the lack of Jewish response in the earlier years. Gradually it became clear that the hope Great Britain had had, as the Mandatory Power for Palestine, of peacefully evolving a bi-national independent state in the country would have to be abandoned. The 'troubles' in Palestine in the years 1933 to 1948 made it clear that extreme Arab Nationalists would not accept this aim for the country. The idea of partition, although fully explored, had also to be given up, and there is no need here to discuss it.

It is certain, however, that Arab nationalism evoked Jewish nationalism. The experience of the Jewish colonists under the British mandate raised serious doubts on whether they could accept the old position of being a permanent minority in a Palestine which had an Arab-dominated government. We must accept the fact that these Jewish colonists had full knowledge of the persecutions endured by their people in past centuries ; that they themselves had had to suffer acutely because of antisemitism ; and that Hitler's Jew-hatred had caused some six million Jews to perish in Europe. Security was what they longed for. The desire to live their own life dominated them. These were urges which could not be denied. These remnants of European Jewry looked back on Hitler, looked at Arab intransigence, and said—'Never again'. This attitude was behind many of the happenings in Palestine in the last years of the British Mandate. Their experiences since coming to the country did not lead the half million Jews there to cultivate patience or moderation. It did make them determined not to submit willingly to a new minority status. Their 'National Home', however limited in scope its planners might have envisaged it, had to become a reality.

Thus it came about that, simultaneously with the giving up by Great Britain of the Mandate for Palestine in May 1948, the new Jewish State of Israel was proclaimed, and the Arab-Israel war of 1948-9 begun. For the Jews this was a war for survival. The Arab League States had made it clear that it was their intention to drive the Israeli forces into the sea and maintain an Arab Palestine. It was a bitter struggle. The Jewish viewpoint is still that they were miraculously aided. At any rate they defeated their northern and southern opponents and fought a drawn battle with those from the east. They survived the year of war and established their State of Israel with the loss of a large area of Arab Palestine to Trans-Jordan and a tiny part to Egypt.

## PROBLEMS TO BE FACED

Inevitably, with the emergence of the new State in this modern world, there were tremendous problems to be faced. These were not only political and economic. There were problems inherent in the fact that this was a *Jewish* state—problems arising from the past of the Jewish people and of those who had fought for the new independence. Many of these problems are incapable of speedy solution and will remain for decades. It is one of the great difficulties in writing of the new State of Israel that too often the rule of expediency has had to be applied to meet this situation or that, and it is very easy to be led astray by what is actually a temporary phase in the present condition of the country and people. We have to remember that (at the time of writing) the State is only in its sixth year of existence. One cannot admire too much the courage and determination of the men who have guided the State thus far, nor grudge them the success which has been theirs in keeping the ship of state afloat ; but most of their problems are such that, at present, one can only state the elements composing them. The solution cannot be given, for it must be spun out of the future corporate life and thought of the Israeli people— and even that corporate life and culture, that ' Israeli ' nationhood, has yet to be won !

It is unfortunate that many people assume that the new Jewish State of Israel will correspond to their ideas of Jews as they have known them in their own country. We have to face the fact that the present population of Israel—some 1,750,000—is 89 per cent Jewish and that these Jews are drawn from all the continents. They have brought with them their national backgrounds—principally Christian or Moslem—and the adults at any rate, will not find it easy to shed their thought forms and habits. Their children, born in Israel, will find it easier but there is as yet no definite Israeli culture for these children to absorb. Education in Israel is still too much the instrument of the political parties, and even the latest arrangement to bring all schools under the Ministry of Education does not entirely remove education from the political sphere. The early language difficulty in the new State—of Jews being unable to talk to each other—is now well on the way to being overcome but it will be long enough before modern Hebrew (new to the majority) bears fruit in a new literature which will express the new culture of the new nation. Here again it is too easy to assume that the old literature, drama, and music of the Jews of the dispersion can be taken over by the new State. It may—as a starting point ! It cannot express the sense of miracle which is in the new nation as a result of its first year of life and war, nor the sense of struggle and achievement against heavy odds which has gone on since that year, nor the sense of the task which lies ahead— the romance of a desert to be conquered and of a new people to be resettled and re-established in the old home.

There are epic possibilities in the theme—but will this congeries of Jews gathered from the ends of the earth be able to forget their individualism and work for the common end of a new Israel with a new destiny ? This is what they must do, but that future and that destiny have to be worked out and there are no very hard and fast lines which can be laid down for this working out by the present rulers in Israel.

There are, of course, those within and without the new State who would wish to lay down definite lines for its development. The most important is the influence of the group of thoroughly Orthodox Jews in the country, a group whose number has been variously estimated but which certainly is less than twenty-five per cent of the total Jewish population. Many Jews inside and outside Israel looked for the new State developing along theocratic lines—a Torah state. Such men ignored the fact that the Wall of the Law was a defensive mechanism to protect Jewish national existence when the Jews were a minority in every country in the world, and that this main function is useless in a Jewish sovereign state, and worse than useless in such a state in the modern world. The orthodoxy of the Ghetto did not have to cope with the maintenance of a modern state : the religious laws that nourished and protected the Judaism of the Diaspora can be an embarrassment once nationhood has been attained. Zionism had its own ideas for the future of the new State. They were realist ideas but with full acknowledgment of the place of Jewish history and religion. Inevitably narrow orthodoxy and Zionism could not agree in regard to the character and future of the new Israel. I think it true to say that the majority of Jews in Israel, and certainly the most influential, are those who were freely accepted as equal citizens in the democracies of the West. In general they maintained their connection with the Synagogue and preserved their Jewish tradition, but for them their religion was thought of in terms from which the political content of a community was banished. They shared in the struggle for social justice—were, indeed, often leaders—and shared the sense of mutual responsibility, which is a part of Judaism, with

6

their non-Jewish fellow citizens. Admittedly their experience was not that of all Jews everywhere, but this was
part of the heritage which they brought into the new
Israeli State.

The breach between the founders of the new Israel and
the Orthodox Group was early evident. In the orthodox
position there is an inheritance from the past which is
incompatible with present-day conditions. The orthodox
leaders are aware of this but the course of events has
shown them to be very tenacious of their views and
willing to give only grudgingly whatever concessions could
be wrung from them. There has also been little sign of
compromise on the Zionist side. Nevertheless the orthodox
and the not-so-orthodox are now thrown together in a
situation where they *must* come to an understanding and
hammer out a *modus vivendi*. When both groups were
minorities outside Israel there was no real need for such
understanding, for both had urgent duties to perform.
Now the socialist welfare State idea and orthodoxy stand
opposed.

Everyone admits that the State is at root religious but the
fact remains that in Israel, as in the dispersion, the Jews are
largely secular. So far as Israel is concerned it shares the
same dilemma as the Christian and Moslem states do—for
all are primarily secular in their activity although they cannot be said to have rejected or forfeited the roots out of which
they have grown. These are inextricably intertwined with
religious values and with ethical values whose roots lie in
religious history. It does seem clear that in Israel Orthodoxy
must recover the flexibility and sensitivity which marked
Rabbinic Judaism in its creative centuries. A solvent must
be found to blend the defensive and romantic Judaism of
the past diaspora period with the background ideas of a
modern State in this modern world. Already there are
signs that many Jews, coming from countries with a Christian
background, find the orthodox Jewish background of the
new State intolerable. Increasingly, Orthodoxy in the new
State will find that it cannot retreat into an ivory tower
however difficult the political compromises before it may

seem. The genius of Judaism inevitably thrusts on Orthodoxy direct political activity. It may be that, until it finds
a spiritual basis of change, it will fight for its rigidity.
Compromise — or better, reformation — seems to be
inevitable.

The really important factor here is that, since liberal
Judaism plays little or no part in Israeli life, the main
alternatives have, so far, been Orthodoxy or secularism—a
secularism with an unorganized and often incoherent sense
of a religious destiny. The surface cock-sureness and
secularism of the mass of the population should not blind
us to the very real, and deep, religious humility that is part
of their inheritance as Jews. But the non-orthodox Jew in
Israel has shown in these past five years that he is not
willing to be dictated to by the ' religious bloc ' except on
elementary matters like the Sabbath as a public day of rest,
and ' kosher ' food. Even in these matters he is fully alive
to the fact that the Rabbinate, while recognizing that such
basic services as water, electricity, the telephone, and the
telegraph must be maintained seven days a week, cannot
bring itself to give the necessary dispensation to orthodox
Jews, and that this results in a rabbi-sanctioned division
of the population into ' observers ' and ' non-observers '.
Nevertheless, the Israeli Jew is proud of the social traditions
of his people and is eager to develop these farther along
modern lines. He is convinced that, now that he is ' just
like other people ' with a country of his own, he is able to
manage his own affairs with efficiency and justice. The
problem which has to be solved is, therefore, that of the
challenge of the non-observing Jew, who is in the majority
in Israel, to the Orthodox bloc. At present in the struggle
the orthodox have lost several open battles but, for economic
and political reasons, continue to enjoy important authority
and influence in various government departments. One
wonders how long this state of affairs will continue. Already
it is clear to the western mind that the orthodox in power
are ready to repeat the mistakes made by many earnest
and convinced Christian protestants in the past in their
endeavours after a uniformity which they deem to be the

Will of God.  They are rigid and narrow, with no political experience, and they draw their support mainly from the Jews with an eastern European or oriental background. The difficulties of complete Sabbath observance, of ' kosher ' food, of religious festivals, and orthodox religious observance in a modern State are being felt by the vast majority with either a sense of impatience or of growing hostility.  The Knesset has been very diplomatic in this matter, probably afraid of wrenching the State apart, and the result has been a series of compromises between secular and sacred.  There is as a result a feeling after the spirit and against the letter of the law—not that this feeling should be exaggerated. It is, however, there.  Orthodoxy is on trial.  It must either find a spiritual basis for change to meet the circumstances of the new day or it must become an anachronism and, if it survives at all, be without any real religious influence on the life of the future Israeli nation, whatever its influence may be on the continuing diaspora.  That would be tragic but it is not likely to come to pass.  The spiritual basis for change will emerge in time.


## THE TASK OF THE CHURCH

It is here that the Christian Church may be able to help. When one examines the position of the Christians in Israel there does not seem much room for optimism as regards the task of evangelizing Israel.  Christians in Israel are, at present, a very tiny minority—a mere two and a half per cent of the total population.  These Christians are drawn from Roman Catholic and the various Orthodox and Protestant Churches.  There has, so far, been little impact on the mass of the Jewish population, for the various Christian bodies are small and scattered and of no great strength.  Moreover, the Roman Catholic and the Orthodox Churches have contented themselves with looking after their Christian communities, religious foundations, and the various historic religious sites, without any special effort in the direction of Jewish evangelism.  The Protestant Churches have made definite efforts, as missionary Churches, to evangelize Jew and Moslem as well as look after those of their own communion. In present-day Israel this effort to evangelize—to offer the Gospel to Jew and Moslem—is still part of the purpose of the existence of these Churches in the State.

It has to be emphasized, however, as it has been clearly pointed out to the Jewish authorities, that what the Christian Church understands by ' evangelism ' is very far from the connotation which the Jew attaches to the word ' proselytism '—a word he uses constantly in his references to Christian life and work. The Jews in Israel, as elsewhere, are anti-missionary and object to any inducements being held out to Jews to embrace Christianity. They also, thinking back in their history, object to any compulsion being applied to Jews to become even nominal Christians. This last is, of course, quite impossible in Israel where the Jews have made their own laws—but it is just as impossible as a policy to the Christian Church. Equally abhorrent to the Church is the idea of encouraging ' rice-Christians '. To the Christian Church ' evangelism ' is the offer to share the riches which came through Jesus Christ with those who do not yet have them. It is an offer to share which may be accepted or rejected. The ideal of religious freedom, which is embodied in the deposited constitution of the State of Israel, is one which has not yet received the imprimatur of the Knesset. It is the practice to allude to this freedom of religion as if it were a foundation stone of the constitution but it is still an ideal.

One must be patient with the Israeli State in this matter. The defensive mind of the Orthodox bloc persists even when now in their own Jewish state. They cannot yet conceive that the Christian Church only asks what it has given for centuries—religious freedom that is real. In Great Britain, North America, and much of Europe there has been no deterrent for a century at least to Judaism again becoming a missionary faith. Ever since the first century, when the Jewish ' Church ' ceased to be missionary and went on the defensive, it has been unable to understand that its defensive mechanism of the Law has been a handicap. Today in Israel, while there may be official toleration and freedom for Christianity, it is a freedom within limits. There is toleration for the Christian minister who works for and within his Christian community; for the Christian hospital which works for the good of the Israeli people and in collaboration with the health authorities; for the Christian school which draws its pupils from the Christian community; but for any effort of the Christian Church outwith these categories there is opposition and criticism, open or concealed. The fact that certain Jews are interested in the story of Jesus and wish to discuss, even academically, Christianity is not yet allowed for. Nor is the fact that, in the present state of education in Israel, there are Jews who wish their children to have their education in a Christian school because of the background and discipline which that education gives.

What do the Orthodox bloc fear? Is it that, having experience of how little hold orthodox Judaism has on the mass, they fear the appeal of Christianity? Or is it the continuation of the protective spirit of the centuries? Or is it that, for the moment at any rate, Judaism has no message for its own people in their present circumstances and in this day and time? If it is the first they have but to look on a similar problem in Christian countries—the Jew will not come into the Christian fellowship, any more than the Gentile will, unless there is something in that fellowship that he desires, that draws him, without which he cannot go on. Christianity does not compel submission, however compelling the fellowship may be when found. As for any idea of protection for the new Israeli, it is bad psychology—the new Jew in Israel has freedom in his own state and must stand for, and by, that freedom in all things—especially those of the mind and spirit. If, however, it is that meantime the rabbis have no vital message for their own people which will bring about a revival of vital religion in their people, and urge them to take their place and make their witness for the eternal values in Judaism, it is a serious situation indeed.

It is just here that the Christian Churches conceive they can help Israel. In such help as can be offered, there is no feeling of superiority, but a searching after eternal truth. Whatever one may think of God's dealings with mankind the fact remains that, after centuries of exile, Jewry has returned to the land of Israel and re-established the state which was crushed with the fall of Jerusalem in A.D. 70. One may quote from the prophets, one may look for Messiah, one may interpret that return in a multitude of ways, but the fact and the future of the State remain and with it the question—What is God working out here ? I do not think anyone has, or can, make up his or her mind on the question. Those who refuse to see the hand of God in history may point to the inevitability of the return (and it is indeed an aspect of it) for the safety of Jewry. There are those in Jewry who, seeing the return to Palestine before the advent of Messiah, boldly claim that the returned nation *is* Messiah. But there are also those who see in this return further questions as to the destiny of Israel. What will the Jewish genius in the new State evolve for the rest of mankind ? Is it accident or design that the three great monotheistic faiths are now centred around Jerusalem ?

Viewing the difficulties, economic, social, medical, educational, and religious, there were many ways in which the Christian Churches already represented in Israel could, and still can, help the new State. In medical, educational, social, and religious work that help has been freely given and, in some cases, at considerable sacrifice. It has been given, however, without prejudice to the missionary tasks of the Church. Where Jews have enquired about Christianity they have been answered, where they have asked for the New Testament it has been given, where they have invited discussion on Christ and Christianity they have been met. There is evident among many enquirers an impatience with the legalistic view of religion and a desire for a more spiritual view, but there are still barriers to the free discussion of religion because of the defensive attitude of mind of the majority of Jews.

One sees this in the attitude to Jewish-Christians.

Officially they are free, unofficially there are all sorts of discriminations practised, and there are many who are undeclared Christians because of this attitude—however much we may deprecate their refusal to declare themselves. It is a matter for great regret that so many of the Jewish Christians left Palestine when Great Britain gave up the Mandate in May 1948 and have not returned. At present their number in Israel is certainly not more than two hundred. The hope of an indigenous Israeli Christian Church is thus on the very far horizon. In the circumstances, and despite the handicaps on evangelism, there is nothing the Christian Churches can do in Israel save accept the opportunities which come their way and especially to meet the needs of the younger generation.

For that younger group in Israel the period of perfervid nationalism is past. They are now searching for new religious forms to give meaning to their new nationhood. They observe the religious festivals, and feast and fast in accordance with the Jewish calendar. Nevertheless they state very definitely that the law-bound Judaism of the Diaspora cannot satisfy them. In the Bible they recognize principles of ethics and morals on which they think they can construct a way of life which is more satisfying than that of the rabbis. The traditions of their people they revere. They recognize that these traditions are necessary for each and every nation. In their own case, however, they look on the traditions the Orthodox would have them accept and say—these derive from the Ghetto period and cannot be accepted by the modern Israeli who is a free man in a free and sovereign state.

There is today a triangle of forces in Israel : the doggedly conservative elderly orthodox shaking their heads at careless youth which rejects their way of life and seeks a new meaning in the old festivals and holidays ; the Zionist pioneers with a secularism that has borne its fruit and now seems to youth to be sterile ; and youth. These young people fought for their State under the inspiration of Zionism but that inspiration, and the leadership which it fostered, are not the same under the new State conditions as in the day of conflict. The urge of conflict has not been transmuted into the new conditions and the simple Zionist Gospel of work, however right, does not meet their spiritual hunger. It has left the youthful idealist searching for a new source of inspiration. Zionism for many does not work any more and they do not know what to put in its place. They only feel, as other groups do, that the State has failed them ; they have not yet exactly fathomed why. The situation is indeed extraordinarily complex. I am unable here to deal with the machinery of government, with the economic problems and difficulties of the new State, with the political questions of the relations with the Arab countries around, the development of the Negev and the plan to increase the Jewish population of Israel to some four million. All these, and many other factors, have their repercussions on the individuals in the Israeli economy. There is a certain sense of disillusionment amongst the inhabitants, and especially (as one would expect) amongst youth. They see Tel Aviv choc-a-bloc with new immigrants from Europe who prefer peddling in the streets to undertaking hard, manual, pioneer work in the settlements or in the Negev. They find themselves up against the attitude of the Jew who, from the comfort of Great Britain, or the U.S.A., or other countries is ready to support financially and with his voice the new Jewish State but who will not emigrate to prove his belief in that State with his person and his work. The problem of a dual loyalty for Jews in other lands than Israel is thus tending to move into a new phase. It is not now a question for the British, American, or other Jew—can I serve two masters, my own country and Israel ? It is a question whether the Israeli Jew should not sever all relations with non-Israeli Jews. Admittedly this problem may never finally arise, but it has been raised and discussed. There is also the group of Jewish immigrants whose disillusionment is so great that they wish to leave Israel and live once again as a minority amongst non-Jews.

It is in this spiritual vacuum created by the Rabbinate that the Christian Church must find its real task. There is a spiritual hunger in the Israeli which must be satisfied.

It may be that what the Christian Church has to offer cannot satisfy the Israeli need, or it may be that the Christian Church will not have full freedom to make its offer (as at present). In any case the offer must be made by the Church and how it works out in the end is a matter for God under whom we, and the Jews, are humble workers. If the Church accepts the opportunity before it—and it has not done so until now—there is a witness to be borne in Israel and a witness which must be made collectively and in co-operation. The Christian institutions remaining to us—whether churches, hospitals, clinics, schools, bookshops, or any other—must be manned by all the Churches witnessing for Christ. Whether any liaison with the Orthodox or Roman Catholic Churches in Israel can be made or maintained is not known to the writer. The necessity for such co-operation in the work in Israel is, at present, the paramount consideration. There is a manifest task laid on the Church of Christ, a plain piece of work to be done and a limited time in which to achieve it, and the Church of Christ must accept the full responsibility for failure to do what is its plain duty. It may be, of course, that orthodox power in Israel will deny to the inhabitants the possibility of deciding for themselves whether the Christian contribution to the upbuilding of the final Israeli State is a valid one or not—but that decision is not in our hands.

# V

# STATE AND RELIGION IN THE STATE OF ISRAEL

### Hans Kosmala

THE State of Israel owes its emergence to the idea of political Zionism and the decision of the United Nations to partition Palestine among Jews and Arabs. Nevertheless, a Jewish State would never have come into existence, much less preserved its life, on the strength of a political idea and an international agreement alone, had there not been two factors on which it could rely in the hour of its birth and afterwards : the colonization of the country and its defence. It is well to remind the reader outside Israel of this fact, the significance of which no one in Israel would deny, not even the opponents of the present Government.

Ever since the first *halutsim*, or pioneers, went out from Russia and Poland to settle in Palestine some seventy years ago in order to found colonies and transform waste-land, covered with stones and thistles, into fertile farms and gardens, new generations of Jews have arisen with a new sense, a new appreciation of the essentials of a full human life, of freedom and independence, of equality, brotherhood and co-operation, of honest productive work and love of the land on which they have laboured, the ancient land of their fathers which has finally become their own. It was during the recent war of independence, and the years preceding it, that they realized that the land would be their own only so long as they were able to defend it.

It is therefore not surprising that the programme of the Government of Israel has two main objects : the building up of the country, in the first place of its agriculture, and the increase and education of a people which is able both to

create new values and to defend them. No one will mini-
mize the importance of these objects, when taking into
account (1) that Israel is still in a state of armed truce with
all its neighbours who do not recognize it as an independent
State, and (2) that its Jewish population has increased
since the proclamation of the State (14th May, 1948) by
more than 100 per cent, from about 650,000 to 1,473,868
(30th Sept., 1953) ; all these immigrants must be inte-
grated as quickly as possible into the household of the new
State, for tens of thousands of them came into the country
with empty hands.

As colonization of the country involves military defence,
so military training cannot serve its purpose unless the young
soldier has at the same time been instructed and trained in
agricultural labour. This, at least, is the view of military
experts, which is now underlying the Government scheme.
Agricultural training as part of army life will facilitate the
establishment of frontier settlements which must serve as the
first wall of defence. This arrangement is only part of a
wider programme. ' As the State cannot order its citizens
to become pioneers and to settle down on the land, or even
near the frontiers, it will have to be the task of the schools
to rear a generation of pioneers who will make it their
sacred duty to revive the desert, to master the elemental
powers, and to create in the Jewish homeland a community
and a civilization which will become a guide-post to the
exiled children of Israel and an example to the whole
world ' (Ben Gurion). The system of *gadna*, the pre-military
service of the secondary school age-group in cadet corps,
will be considerably extended so as to embrace the majority
of the young people, in order to secure leaders for the future.
*Gadna* subjects are included in the syllabus of the schools.
Groups of young immigrants leave their camps and attend
an intensive course of training and study in which they
are made familiar with the life of the country and the
duties they have to perform in the service of the nation.
Some of these youths return to their camps as *gadna*
instructors.

In order to achieve their aim, the leaders of the nation

must first win the youth, inspire it with their ideals, and train it accordingly. Old people rarely change the course to which they are accustomed. Considering that the immigrants come from different parts of the world and have brought with them their different ways of life, not to mention the astounding ' racial ' differences between the various groups in spite of the fact that they all are Jews, we cannot but wonder how these different peoples can ever become one nation with a common national code of life. How can a Jew educated in the cultured milieu of the Central European countries, of Britain, or America, feel and think in common with his new fellow-citizens hailing from the small towns of Morocco, of Yemen, of the plains of the Euphrates, or the highlands of Kurdistan ? Not in this generation, anyway.

The Government believes it has found the remedy for the future : it is the Army, Israel's defence and pioneer force with all its ramifications, which is to become the ' melting-pot ' of the nation. The present leaders of the State have this vision and the hope that it will come true. ' The law of Israel was founded upon a code of ordinances, of what to do and what not to do. So the commandment to act is essential in Judaism : the law of action is the law of *halutsiut* (pioneering) ' (Ben Gurion). No doubt, young people, even if they come from different quarters, can be welded together into one working unit by occupational and mental training. This has been done before.

However, we need not wonder that this new national ' code of life ' has been severely criticized in various Jewish groups in and outside Israel as inconsistent with the Jewish spirit : indeed, it has been admitted in official circles that the new trend involves a revaluation of the Jewish values of the past. Many, especially the older Zionists, fear that the ' glorification of the Israeli as a fighter ' will lead to a ' Pagan apotheosis of the warrior ' and that therefore Israel's Army should never be made ' the chief expression of reborn Jewishness '. ' This is not what the Jewish people, or Judaism, survived for. This is not what the Zionist movement intended, and what Israel and Judaism should

in Jewish religious law, and there are therefore no provisions for such a State of the Jews—with one exception perhaps : the regulations concerning the Gentiles travelling through or sojourning in the land at the time of Jewish autonomy (Maimonides, Mishne Torah, Hilch. Akum x : 6). Jewish tradition knows only of two Golden Ages, one half mythical : in the past under King David and King Solomon, and the other at the end of the days, the kingdom of the Messiah. Strictly speaking it is the Messiah who will bring the scattered Jewish people from the four ends of the earth back to the Promised Land. He will be the sovereign king of Israel and will subdue the nations, and all will recognize him as their Lord and become God-fearers.

That will happen sometime in the future when ordinary history will end. Extreme orthodoxy cannot, therefore, and does not recognize the present State of Israel, but it is only a small minority who refuse to have anything to do with this ' godless ' State. Most orthodox groups do collaborate with the State and even participate in its Government, though not unconditionally. Holding on to their orthodox principles of faith, they consider it their main object to introduce as many religious laws as possible. So far they have succeeded in having three main groups of laws recognized and more or less generally observed : *kashrut* (dietary laws), Sabbath observance, and religious marriage. When the new orthodox Mayor of Jerusalem was introduced to his office in 1952 he declared that ' the primary concern of the Orthodox bloc is the guarding of traditional education ', and that ' he is pledged to do everything in his power to enforce the by-laws relating to Sabbath observance ' (*Jerusalem Post*, Oct. 27, 1952). Sometimes religious customs are introduced or ancient feasts revived. In the year 1952 the assembly mentioned in Deut. xxxi : 10 ff, which had not been called together for about 1900 years, was re-instituted by the Ministry of Religion. Another sign of orthodox confidence in the future may be seen in the resolution to erect a three-storey building for the offices of the Chief Rabbinate in Jerusalem at a cost of just under half a million dollars ; but there is yet no indication of a revival of the Sanhedrin, the ancient religious court of justice, which is demanded by many religious Jews who are hoping for an early clarification of the relationship between religion and the State. The leaders of orthodoxy do not seem to be in a hurry, because the formation of the Sanhedrin at the present time might not, or not yet, secure a constitution they would favour.

Orthodox leadership has been accused from all quarters of attaching more importance to questions of Jewish ritual than to the most elementary requirements of public weal. Criticisms come even from within ; but when a speaker of a progressive orthodox group in a recent orthodox meeting declared that ' religion does not consist in *kasher* meat and ritual bath only ', he was shouted down with the cry : ' Apostate ! ' Arguments of a more fundamental nature have been brought forward by Professor Isaiah Leibowitz, himself the founder of the Religious Workers' Group within the Jewish Labour Movement (*Histadrut*). He pointed out that religious Jews have entangled themselves in inconsistencies and contradictions which are detrimental to the character and the honour of the Torah, for they can observe the traditional law only at the price of a conscious approval of religious transgression by the State and the nation as a whole. On the Sabbath they use electricity (by means of an automatic switch which does the work for them) and water provided by communal works, which are run by other Jews. They approve of the functioning of the police on the Sabbath, of Israel shipping, of military service for girls, provided the work is done by the sons and daughters of other Jews. Tacitly they admit the need for all such functions contrary to the provisions of the Law, they vote for them in Parliament and avail themselves of the necessaries supplied by State and community, but at the same time attack the State and its Government for their transgression of the Law.

Many orthodox Jews wait for the Rabbinical authorities to show the way out of the dilemma, for rabbis could assume the right to promulgate new decisions of such a kind as to answer, to some extent at least, the needs of nation and

7

State. Why do they hesitate ? Is it lack of initiative ? The reason for their hesitation is, so it seems, that a new and adequate rabbinic legislation would have to annul many of the established laws which are made absolute by the faith in the tradition from Mount Sinai and are sanctified by the blood of martyrs who died for this faith. It may be easy for us to ask them to surrender ' the service of the letter ' and to follow the spirit of God's Torah—but not for them to do so.

Be this as it may, the present orthodox position seems untenable. The cry of responsible Jewish men and women for a renewal of Jewish religion becomes louder with every year of Israel's independence. Professor Leibowitz believes that ' the future of Judaism as religion rests on the initiative of the community of religious workers, farmers, soldiers, and servants of the State ' (cf. his article in *Jerusalem Post*, Sept. 19, 1952). Others again complain of the indifference and indolence of a large part of the Jewish population, who have lost all interest in religion as they know it. It is true, the Bible is still read in Israel—in the first place as literature and a book of Jewish history. Similarly, the interest in the history and the archaeology of the country probably beats all records in other countries : one out of every 600 Jewish adults (over 20 years) is a member of the Israel Exploration Society (October 1952). Under the auspices of the Hebrew University and the Ministry of Education, university and school teachers conferred together in April 1952 in order to discuss the position of the Bible (Old Testament) in the national and cultural education of Jewish youth. The left-wing groups held their own convention six months later and demanded a new approach to the Bible as a secular cultural heritage, which was to supersede the ' religious and idealistic conception of the Bible ' still prevalent. Curiously, there are in Israel Marxists who would exempt the Bible from materialistic criticism.

We find today many leaders in Israel with a multitude of ideas and suggestions for an intellectual and religious renewal, but there is as yet no prophet with a message. Meanwhile the Government pursues its programme.

Christians outside Israel will now be anxious to know what place the Christian religion takes in the life of the Jewish nation. The answer to the question can be brief : the role of the Christian Church as a spiritual force among the Jewish population of Israel is negligible. The position of the Churches and of Christian work in Israel has been dealt with in a separate chapter. Suffice it here to say that Christians, also Christians of Jewish origin, may worship in complete freedom in the established Churches or in private houses. The numbers of people attending Sunday services (especially in such larger towns as Tel-Aviv, Haifa, Jerusalem, and Tiberias) vary from half a dozen up to about seventy or eighty. Gentile Christians visiting Jerusalem are offered an invitation to the weekly united Christian prayer meetings at the official Israel Tourist Bureau, if the tactful officer in charge (a rabbi) finds it appropriate. All active missionary work among the Jews is disliked—although not prohibited. That is the official attitude. If the zeal of a missionary attracts the attention of eager orthodox youths, it may sometimes happen that they try and take the law of Moses into their own hands (see *e.g. Jerusalem Post*, Oct. 15, 1952), thus infringing the law of the State. The liberal-minded, as a rule, consider missionaries harmless. There is no Christian literature that would appeal to intelligent Jews. Bibles, with and without the New Testament, and in the various (over 30) languages spoken in Israel, find a ready market. There is no Protestant press in Israel. Jews, with very rare exceptions, do not attend Christian services : Christianity in its ecclesiastical form does not attract them. There is, however, a small Hebrew Christian (largely Rumanian) congregation in Haifa under the leadership of a minister of the Norwegian Church (formerly in Rumania). On the other hand, it is a noteworthy fact that interest in Jesus—not the Christ, but Jesus, the man who was born a Jew and denounced by the Synagogue—has rather increased than diminished. Considering the shortage of paper and foreign currency we are surprised at the number of books on Jesus and Christianity published in the last few years in Israel. Among the

historical works we must mention the German edition of
Josef Klausner's *From Jesus to Paul* (Jerusalem, 1950) and
the new) third) edition, also in German, of *Jesus of Nazareth*
(Jerusalem, 1952).   Large sections of his Hebrew work on
the *History of the Second Temple*, especially in volumes 4 and 5
(Jerusalem, 1950 ff), deal with the beginnings of Christianity.
'The Rise of the Christian Religion' is the subject of a
study by A. Z. Marcus (Hebrew, Jerusalem, 1950), who
makes ample use of quotations from the New Testament.
Josef Hagar's essays on Jesus and his contemporaries were
published under the title *Historical Points of View* (Hebrew,
Tel-Aviv, 1951).   Some of the recent works of Martin
Buber, in which New Testament problems occupy a promin-
ent place, are too well known to need special notice here.

What is even more significant is that the Jewish poets
and thinkers in Israel have repeatedly tried to portray the
character of this ' most problematical figure of the Jewish
history' and, naturally, that of Judas Iscariot.   In the
thirties A. A. Kabak published in Hebrew a Jesus novel
entitled *On the Narrow Path*.   It is the narrow path mentioned
in II Esdras : chapter vii : verses 6–9, which serve as motto to
the book.   The novel was re-issued in 1950.   In the same
year, Max Brod, a prolific and versatile writer and religious
thinker, presented us with his novel *The Master*.   At the
moment not only is the German original in the press in
Europe, but also a Hebrew translation is being prepared
in Israel under a different title (*The Little Sister*), the Hebrew
equivalent, *The Rabbi*, having been found unsuitable for
various reasons.   *Jesus of Nazareth* is the name of a dramatic
tale by Nathan Bistritzki (Hebrew, Tel-Aviv, about 1950).
Finally, H. Hazaz, a modern Hebrew classicist, has for
some time occupied himself with the same subject and his
study of the Nazarene, parts of which have already been
published, may be complete in the near future.

It is interesting to note that Klausner, who is 80, has
retained in all his Hebrew writings the traditional form of
the name, Yeshu, once used by the scurrilous ' Toldoth
Yeshu ' books of the Middle Ages (whereas in all translations
the common Greek form ' Jesus ' has been substituted for

it). Kabak, who would now be 72, did the same. The younger generation, however, seems to prefer the historical and more objective form 'Yeshua', which is the correct Hebrew equivalent of the Greek form of the name.

How does the Jewish public in Israel view the preoccupation with the man Jesus? Those who have received a liberal education seem to welcome such literature, even if it is only for the sake of intellectual freedom. The average Jew with no particular religious background does not mind it, whereas the orthodox Jew usually resents any literary appreciation of that man and his teaching. The genuine communist, naturally, considers the teachings of Jesus, together with the religion of Jewish orthodoxy, as opium. When Sholem Asch, the well-known American Jewish author, who apart from specifically Jewish novels wrote *Jesus of Nazareth*, *The Apostle*, and *Mary*, visited Israel in spring 1952, he was hailed by all advocates of intellectual freedom, whilst an orthodox paper stigmatized him as a 'traitor', as one 'who sold his pen and honour for gain of money and a halo of fame in the Christian world, who is singing songs of praise for a religion which oppresses the religion of Israel' (*Hamodia*, April 23, 1952).

Instead of drawing any conclusions from the observations recorded in this brief account of State and religion in Israel today, or even prognosticating future developments, the writer would rather content himself with cautioning Christian people against exaggerated and one-sided reports on the state of religion in Israel or certain religious developments. Such descriptions are often based less on facts than on hopes and wishes, or on disappointments; sometimes they emphasize particular circumstances and lose sight of other no less important facts and events. We must beware of rash conclusions in whichever direction they may tend, remembering that we are today not nearer the Kingdom of God than at the time of the apostle Paul—and not farther from it either. 'Let us watch and be sober . . .' (I Thess. v : 6–8) ; let us judge with understanding and act in sympathy and love, not forgetting that the Jewish people has suffered much from Christian hands.

# VI

# SOME QUESTIONS TO THE CHRISTIAN CHURCH FROM THE JEWISH POINT OF VIEW

## Leo Baeck

Is Judaism entitled, or even bound, to ask Christianity questions, its peculiar Jewish questions, and to claim answers, the genuinely Christian answers—and, of course, to expect the truly Christian questions too ? History, past and present, affirms the right to do so.

We have had nineteen centuries of Christian history, emanating from, and ever anew confronted with, Judaism. And in these centuries Jewish history time and again has encountered, and been encompassed by, Christianity. Inescapably they were, and remain, interrelated.

Moreover, at bottom, Judaism in itself poses a question, a perennial one, to Christianity ; and Christianity in itself poses a question, a permanent one, to Judaism. They are a problem each to the other. Neither is really able to vindicate itself without having truly heard the other.

Yet, for all that, when throughout the centuries have Judaism and Christianity looked each other full in the face ? When did they frankly, honestly converse—frankly, wishing and daring to speak of the soul of the faith, the very heart of the belief ; honestly, with that sympathy which is essential to human understanding ?

Usually, if there was some discussion, Christianity from the first assumed that it had the final answer, and Judaism shunned, or was afraid of, approaching the final questions. There was scarcely any true debating. And the usual, and inevitable, result of any talk was an increase in the feeling, on the Christian side, of being uncompromisingly rejected by the Jew, and, on the Jewish side, of being forcibly summoned and violently accused by the Christian—let alone the fact of the restrictions and burdens imposed on the Jew by, or on behalf of, the Church.

It would not serve any purpose here to enlarge on this. What matters, and should concern both Judaism and Christianity today, is the present way and the present duty, the problem of the actual approach. Certainly, ' there is a time to keep silence, and a time to speak '. But now, it seems, is the season for speaking. On us today, it seems, is laid a solemn obligation that the Jewish and Christian faiths meet openly—faiths indeed, not only boards or writers or orators. It may turn out one day a sin of omission if they carelessly or timidly or presumptuously shrink from asking and answering the right questions. But if they gain mutual comprehension, the task could prove one day ' even a blessing in the midst of the land '—and may in the long run also help in uprooting this antitheism which so successfully goes under the name of antisemitism.

Today our way is already prepared. Everywhere many a soul has opened, self-confidence and self-righteousness have been shaken. There is some self-preoccupation, but a growing interest in the other point of view. People who apparently wished to see the courses diverging now welcome a junction here and there. Moreover, with modern transport, distances on earth diminish, and we are all becoming near neighbours, unable to evade or avoid one another. Willing or not, we learn about one another, share our fears and hopes. There seem to be universal fears and hopes. To some people this can at first mean a painful embarrassment, but it points at such opportunities, such possibilities as can be like messengers sent out by Providence. We should not ignore or disregard them. We should venture on asking questions.

It is, however, essential that these should be genuine questions, asked in the hope of eliciting honest answers. If two men were convinced that a chasm was unbridgeable, they would do no good standing on opposite sides and calling across to one another. If, however, they were convinced that a bridge could and should be built, they would ask one another constructive questions, their best qualities would be brought to the fore, and they would be drawn together by the common task. So with bridging our spiritual division, faith that it can be done draws us together and inspires sincere questioning ; and we shall not forget that there is common ground supporting us both.

The assumption of, indeed the belief in, common ground is indispensable here both psychologically and logically. If the one or the other disclaim or dissemble it, any engaging in questions must remain aimless and fruitless, or could even become prejudicial. He who, standing on the common ground, is prepared to ask his questions is fully aware, and supposes the other likewise to be, that between them there are differences that denote unequivocal and unimpeachable distinctions. He does not want them to be repressed or concealed or belittled on either side. But he is certain, and trusts the other side to be certain, that even these differences have their deepest roots in and owe their very existence to this common ground. Unless he is conscious of this, he will not really understand the differences either.

And now, which are these questions that Judaism is in such a spirit allowed, and even obliged, to ask the Church ? They will not be designed to challenge dogma or articles of faith : the other's creed is his sanctuary that cannot be queried or disputed here. The subject of our questions is not the ' what ' but the ' how ' ; that is to say, not the belief in itself, in its contents, but so to speak the conduct of the belief—not what the belief wants to say, but how it is saying it. Every religion claims its place and asserts its task in the world. It also wishes to strengthen this place and to confirm this task. It cannot dispense with it. Our problem is not this incontestable effort of every religion, but is quite a different one. It is the problem of the manner and the style. There is a well-known French saying, ' Le style c'est l'homme '. ' The style is the man ', and one could emphatically add : the religion, too.

This is, therefore, the first question here : What is the manner, the style, of the Church when in its indisputable striving for its place and task in the world, it meets with others, in our case with the Jewish religion and the Jewish sphere ? Does it take the truly religious course, that which is directed by a genuine pious feeling ? Or does there, more or less distinctly, appear here another motive, another sentiment and desire ? One could put it also thus : Is the approach, or perhaps even an attack, made here out of a sincere belief or only in the interest of a belief ?

History explains what is meant by this. In former days, as the Jew sees it, the Churches represented political rather than religious bodies and systems. They seemed to marshal themselves against him, intent on domination. He looked upon them as part of the trying circumstances with which he constantly had to come to terms. The perennial religious problem, with all that it embraced, receded far into the background, where only some conspicuous points were incidentally perceived. Not a religious agent, not a pious hopefulness, but this hard force and heavy influence exerted by the Churches impressed themselves upon the Jew time and again—let alone the fact that the Churches used to sit in judgment on the Jew like God's counsellors and to pass on him final sentences, at best to display a kind of condescension.

Days have changed, and manners change, but this question is still alive : When the call of the Church addresses itself to others, to dissenting people like the Jews, and invites them in the name of the Church, whose voice is really heard : the voice of the messenger of the religion or that of an envoy of a régime ?—of the faith only, or of an authority ?

Within the Church itself it is an old problem whether or how far religion can be combined with worldly power. In course of time such power had fallen to the lot of the Churches. Often without, or perhaps against, their wish it had become a fact, a historic one ; never was that problem solved. They who are possessed of power are ever anew threatened by it. Though power seems at first to serve them for a good purpose, it often tends to master them for its own ends. Paradoxically, the proper fight against this power has to be fought out, not by those who are powerless, but by the powerful one himself.

To Judaism it grew to be a heavenly dispensation that it was never mighty on earth—only in the fables of the multitude ; its real and singular strength lies in its patience and vision.  The Church, time and again, was on trial : power tried to prevail over it.  Power may be characteristic of political or economic or social or military formations, and they may glory in it.  But it is contradictory to the character of the community of faith, since it is contradictory to the principle of faith.  The Church is led into temptation here. It is the tempter who says : ' All this power will I give thee '. The word of the Lord is this other one : ' Not by might, nor by power, but by my spirit, saith the Lord of Hosts.' In the long run power will corrupt religion from within.

Therefore, from the Jewish point of view, this is a basic question :  When different religions, say Christianity and Judaism—and the two cannot evade each other today— come to face one another, or if they should one day purposefully convene, will it be like a meeting of the Great Powers, invested with authority and vetoes, and a small country ? Or are they to converse and work with each other as equals because, and for the sake of, a common purpose—equals not in a social but a spiritual sense—and thus neither diverted nor confused by any majority-complex on the one side or any minority-complex on the other ?

In the latter case, hopes and desires will then meet ; and as both have from the beginning been conscious here of the common ground, so they will now be aware of some common outlook.  Without this wide outlook on to that common ground, any meeting, however important, would be an isolated event leading nowhere.  Moreover, in the religious sphere, especially from the Jewish point of view, any question, while starting from the past and the present, has its full truth only when aiming at the days to come.

It is not as a point of debate but in the interests of mutual trust that these genuine questions are asked here.  Such questions never come from one who is satisfied with his own understanding, content to let things take their course—

who thinks he has all the answers firmly bearing him out. Only he who really thirsts after the days of the divine promise is afflicted with the desire to question. This thirst is a constantly active force in the innermost feelings of the religious man. And he is fervently confident that one day all people will be stirred by it, that God ' will send this thirst in the land '.

From the Jewish angle it has sometimes seemed as if the Church was on the side of, or at least sympathized with, the satisfied, and that only in the Jew was there this constant craving of the soul, and that only he could plead the cause of those who thus thirsted. There seemed also to be a reason for it. In the Jewish view the idea of, and belief in, the Kingdom of God as realized and presented by the Church emphasized the miraculous heavenly interposition rather than the constant obligation laid on man to choose and take the stand laid down in the divine commandment. It seemed to the Jew that the Church laid more stress on its early history than on what is to be done today and tomorrow to promote the aims and fulfilment of true human history.

Matters of fact, general and Jewish matters, came forward and did, in themselves, pose questions to the Church. Yet has not the Church, as a whole, extensively or intensively, played an unimportant part in the historic painful endeavours for human liberation and emancipation ? Was it not comparatively late in the day that what others achieved by great exertions and sacrifices was finally somehow acknowledged by the whole of the Church ? And here a special question raises its voice : What, on the whole, was the attitude here, the attitude of mind and action, adopted by the Church when peoples started to right the wrong that for so long had been done to Judaism and to the Jew ?

It will do even more good to turn towards the future and to the problems that may arise there. Debating and reproaching, indeed, will hardly be of use, nor provide a remedy. Only the consciousness of the common outlook will make for a growing awareness of the common way, or at least of a common direction. Of course, sometimes the views or the terms will differ here, and not only matters of method, but those of principle will be the points in question. But just the frank agreeing on differences will prove to be a help and even a means of approach. It will more and more be seen that there can scarcely be a more excellent possibility of honestly coming together, and of really understanding one another, than through this awareness of, not only the common ground, but also a common outlook.

One problem should be touched upon here, the problem of the missionary task, and the way it manifests itself and is carried out. No religion that is conscious of its title, mindful of its vocation, and always certain of having that true future that will vindicate its belief, can resign from this task. And no religion can justly assign this task to itself alone and deny it to another. There may be times or even epochs when somewhere, perhaps everywhere, a religion is faced with doors barred and bolted : as were, for instance, Christianity in the days of the early persecution, or later in the realms of firmly established Islamic domination, and Judaism almost everywhere throughout the long centuries of the Middle Ages and after. But never can genuine religions renounce the obligation of the mission entrusted to them : it is part of their very being as religions, part of their duty to mankind ; nor can they neglect its demands without renouncing their very being and stifling their human character. To be indifferent to this task would here signify some inner weakness and indolence or even a self-centredness contradictory to the religious way.

Therefore—and this also deserves attention—no community of faith has the right to take offence at the other's missionary work or purpose, whatever be the province the other is turning to. There can be no monopolies here, nor reserved regions. But, for the sake of religious purity, one supposition must be confirmed : and from the Jewish angle this implies a question to Christianity. Namely, when in the course of that task people, believers or unbelievers, are invited or approached, who is to address them, who is to step forth and give witness ? Will it be only those moved by the soul of religion, pure faith, and love and trust? Or will there appear also, and perhaps soon take the lead, counsellors of earthly powers and of dominant prejudices, advocates of promising influences and profitable relations?

In former days there was a kind of ecclesiastical imperialism and colonialism, the men of war often laying the foundations. To the Church it meant a recovery and even a renascence when, in recent times, such courses were blocked almost everywhere, though it sometimes seems that here and there some part of the old method has survived, although greatly changed. Not only did allurements display their charm to attract the irresolute and help him in being directed to the easy way, but also a gentle pressure could be employed now and then in order to assist him who still seemed to waver. There were, and on occasion are, many and manifold occurrences, tragic and comic, that make a curious chapter in the history of what is called religion.

And, on the other hand—and this is a further question, which should not be eluded—what of the man who was reclaimed and received? Was he converted or only deserting? Did he with conviction desire to embrace this faith, to profess it uprightly and bravely? Certainly, everyone should hold this man in esteem. Or was he only, or chiefly, desirous of enjoying some advantages now, of gaining entry to certain circles? Everyone surely should hold such a man in contempt. In any case it is the dignity of religion, something therefore common to all to whom religion means the inner reality, which is at stake here.

This dignity must essentially be the hallmark of any relations between Christianity and Judaism; between the two there will be noble relations or no real relations at all. It will also characterize, and give true meaning to, all the questions asked here.

For the sake of this dignity one problem is to be kept in view always. It is the one problem which, obviously, comprehends all the others, the past, the present, and those which are to be. It concerns the crucial point, this decisive point of the lasting actuality and the permanent significance and importance of the Jewish faith, and love, and hope.

It appears to the Jew that, in consequence of misinterpretations or misrepresentations (and they are supposed to be quite honest) of some phrases in the Gospel, the Church did and does proclaim, as it were, an act of attainder against the Jewish religion and those who profess it. One heard, or thought one heard, the Church preach and teach, openly or by insinuation, that any further existence of Judaism is, so to speak, without legitimacy and means a mere arrogation of right, in obstinate defiance of a divine sentence. It was allowed that, in bygone days, prior to the commencement of the new era, Judaism had its singular place and its especial task, its legal title before God and history. But, at a given time, when the great day came that was predestined to mark the turn of all days, that right lapsed, or was forfeited. Since then—such was the inference drawn or implied here—this Jewish people, this people of the Jewish religion, means merely a shadow of history, the dark shadow cast by the past upon the present. It has no real, no living history. It is but a bearer of a religion which has now no present task, no proper aim, and no right to a future of its own.

The picture of Judaism and the Jewish people thus formed seems to show a nation that for many centuries has uneasily and without purpose wandered over the earth, devoid of a fulfilment, destitute of a completion. Led astray by inane thoughts and beliefs, loaded with a burdensome law, it is waiting for what never will arrive—a strange people of a queer frame of mind. A residue of a formerly significant people, it will perhaps be preserved till the day comes for it to bear witness against itself. In such a manner the Jew and his faith were again and again depicted—let alone the fables that used to go the round of the Church. According to the epochs and the fashion of the day, some aspects could vary here, but the main features were well established.

There could be no greater barrier to mutual understanding, or even to honest and heartfelt discussion. It must impede both the Jew and the Christian, the one no less than the other. Such a portrayal can do more harm than any fact, and than any problem.

Of course, everyday life gives rise to rules and its own philosophy. In every day's encounters and affairs the Christian comes across the Jew, and accepts this as a reality that, like other things in life, may or may not prove pleasant. But he does not ask whether history gives him the right to call himself a Jew. He will accept him as such in spite of what the Church has preached and taught. In their respective religious characters also the Christian meets the Jew, perhaps for some common endeavour involving religion. Here again he does not demand that the Jew produce credentials given by history proving that his religion is still an actuality. Daily life often involves convenient evasions ; it moves about the peripheries rather than towards the centre.

But our object here is quite different. It is not that of daily life and its conveniences, but it is concerned with the generation to come and the hope to be realized. Its concern is those long-standing problems which, today and tomorrow, inescapably engage the honest mind, Christian as well as Jewish, problems dominating Jewish life throughout the centuries. Our object, therefore, is to seek religious truth, as far as man on earth is capable of attaining it, by means of a veracity that is prepared to keep to the centre and to strive to ask the right questions and to elicit sincere answers to them.

From this point of view, one question must come foremost : Is the Church really intent on seeing the Jewish religion as it really is and has come to be in virtue of a singular history ? Will the Church recognize this full life that is and has been the essence of Judaism, and that so far as man is capable of foreseeing will remain so from generation to generation ?

Those who are able and sincerely willing to consider the facts and frankly acknowledge them will soon be aware that, if anyone, the Jew has always seen the way clear before him. It was a hard way mostly, and it demanded sacrifices, but it was his way, his own distinctive way, and never was he doubtful that it was shown to him by God. His place was often insecure, but never was he uncertain about the line he had to follow. Perhaps this was the difference between him and men of other nations : that they had an assured place and he had this certainty of the way. He was on the way, indeed, advancing, as creative genius always must, from hope to hope, from prospect to prospect. The realization of the way meant to him more than mere possession. More than any other, he therefore must be considered as the author of true history.

He is to be thus regarded, indeed, because the process of his history was chiefly a spiritual, a religious one. His proper struggle for existence was the struggle for his religious existence, for his spiritual property. There he found the full cogency and thus the entire reality of his life. From this sphere came the sources of his strength, which seemed, and may seem, to be inexhaustible and to make him unconquerable. He was apportioned not a static repose, but a dynamic force which alone enabled him to pursue the way, to 'go from strength to strength' while resisting assault and temptation. Every form of spiritual life, so long as it remains spiritual endeavour, every religion, so long as it remains religious effort, knows its days of trial.

These very days are the essence of their history. Christianity could, and can, experience them. But no one has had to endure such almost incessant trials as Judaism, and in this sense none has so much true history.

Here another fact should also be appreciated by the Church in order to set a just value on Judaism. Such history is mainly a history of renascences. They are the test and the proof of inner vitality. There are periods of self-satisfaction, when this inherent force is suppressed by many external influences ; and in periods of fatigue it can lie dormant. But if there really is this vital power, sooner or later it will come forth, opening men's eyes and leading them to examine both themselves and the changes taking place in the world. It will regenerate the spirit, and people will be conscious and capable of the old task that now has to be performed in a new way to meet the needs of the changed times. The renascences are the testimonies to the vitality of a faith, and thereby a guarantee of its endurance and ability to meet the needs of days to come.

Christianity can point to many a wonderful rebirth and is entitled to take pride in each of them. They are the essence of Christian history. But may they not also be regarded as an inheritance—and not the only one—from the Jewish religion, like that power to withstand trials which is also such a heritage? For the history of Judaism, first and foremost, is characterized, not only by trials steadily endured, but also by renascences and revivals. Rebirth after rebirth, renewed vigour meeting the challenge of a new day, impress upon this history a special significance and give it its own peculiar traits.

Thus it has never been a history of easeful days. There were the travails of the rebirth and the anxieties of the revival. There were the painful compunctions also, and the spiritual and moral conflicts, the crucial divergences in outlook. But, as the storm that had so often blown from without had been weathered, so was the storm that arose within. History kept to its firm course again. Spiritual life was inspired anew, with fresh fullness and vigour. The Church also has experienced this, sometimes in a remarkable manner. Therefore it may well be able to bring understanding and sympathy to the appreciation of this momentous drama of Jewish history, perhaps the most momentous in the record of mankind. There could be no greater contribution to the fruitful exchange of questions and answers, the promotion of mutual understanding.

A historic fact, an important one, can help here to open the way to this understanding. The creed, and indeed the history, of the Church were in a great measure determined by its claiming the Hebrew Bible. From the beginning the Church firmly took possession of it, not only keeping it and giving it new interpretation, but also holding to it and shielding it. The title of the Old Testament had very soon to be fought for against many an adversary, from both within and without. This was the first real trial the Church had to go through and, by withstanding it, it reaffirmed

8

and reassured itself. Moreover, as the Synagogue had translated its Bible into Greek and thus made it a great missionary force sent out to the Greek world, so the Church, by rendering it, together with the New Testament, into Latin, gave it to the Western world that was to gain predominance in Europe.

All this did not merely mean following a given course. It likewise signified going out to meet a true need. It was by virtue of the Old Testament that the Church was able to aim at being the ' *Civitas Dei* ', the City of God, and the ' *communio sanctorum* ', the Communion of the Saints, and at the same time strive to penetrate the sphere of the state and to lay stress upon ' natural law '. One could ponder on whether without the Old Testament the Church had ever lived to see true history. A study of ' Marcionism ' in past and present days affords instructive information bearing on this reflection.

Moreover, another point deserves consideration, a point concerning the New Testament. For this question, too, arises here : What would be the frame and substance of the New Testament, especially of the Gospel, without the Old Testament contained in it : that is to say, if one subtracted from it the Old Testament quotations, direct and indirect ? And supposing one tried to subtract also all that, intentionally or unintentionally, clearly expresses words and thoughts, feelings, hopes and certainties of the Jew in that very land and in those very days ? Perhaps it would be worthwhile to try to envisage the result.

Did the Church—and this is here the question to the Church from the Jewish point of view—always show willingness and readiness to acknowledge these plain facts, to become fully conscious of what they mean, and to confess to their significance ? Has there not been, and is there not apparent now, some laxity and indifference in this regard, at best a sort of so-called neutrality, sometimes a condescension ? Of course, this is not a problem with respect to the Old Testament itself or to Judaism as such. It is a problem that concerns only the Church. And there it is a very critical problem ; there are well-remembered incidents that illustrate it. The Church only can fight its way through it. But, if Judaism is allowed to make observations, and to put its questions to the Church, this surely will be one of them, and not the last nor the least.

The problem the Church is brought up against here is even a deeper one. By virtue of the Bible and of the Jewish heritage as a whole, there are in the Church forceful Jewish elements. They could never be uprooted, nor be repressed for long. They proved to be a strong ferment in the Church, a leaven that permeated and agitated its spiritual life. Epochs were evolved thereby. In a great measure the history of the doctrines that have been striven for within the Church is, one might say, a history of Judaism within the Church. All this is a part of the Jewish drama in the world. Insufficient attention is paid to this phenomenon. But the more the Church becomes aware of it, the more it will become cognizant both of essential elements of its own life and of the unique significance of the survival of the Jewish religion. On the other side, Judaism itself while considering the matter will grow more conscious of its proper peculiarity.

On the whole, both sides will truly benefit by considering all these questions. While questioning Christianity, Judaism must pass on to questions that, in all honesty, it has to put to itself. And Christianity will, vice versa, experience the same compulsion. On both sides new thoughts, new problems will arise and press for new consideration, and each of the two religions will enrich and inspire itself as well as the other. As there has been at least some consciousness first of a common ground and then of a common outlook, there will now grow up an awareness of common problems also.

What has to be presented here is the range of the questions that, from the Jewish point of view, Christianity is to be asked. Judaism is given the right to put these questions, and it is a duty to do so. But it stands to reason that in the same way Christianity is entitled, and morally and religiously obliged, from its specific standpoint to put questions to Judaism. It seems as if formerly there had been too many answers designed only to close the questions, in order that then the one could turn his back upon the other. There were, so it seems, too few questions of the right kind. Such questions call for sincere answers and connote a desire to meditate on these, in order to meet again and honestly question each other anew. We are, it must be repeated, in need of such questionings. They, and only they, could bring an approach that would lead to a real coming together.

Quite an especial blessing will grow from this soil. Self-communion and self-examination will be instigated and encouraged by this questioning as well as by this answering. Inner voices will be heard. To each other Judaism and Christianity will be admonition and warning : Christianity becoming Judaism's conscience, and Judaism Christianity's. That common ground, that common outlook, that common problem which they come to be aware of will call them to make a joint approach.

And then the two will be able to take their stand together, not against one another but side by side, before the Almighty's tribunal, the judgment-seat before which Jew and Christian alike know that man is summoned every day.

# VII

# CO-OPERATION BETWEEN CHRISTIANS AND JEWS

### Its Possibilities and Limitations

#### WILLIAM W. SIMPSON

IT was Easter in the year 1914. Drawn together by what one of them later described as ' an undefined presentiment of catastrophe ' a group of men from several European countries met to discuss the setting up of a supra-national authority in hope of staving off disaster. Considerable progress was made, and agreement reached to convene a larger group in the following August.

' Then,' wrote Martin Buber, the chronicler of that meeting, ' as we discussed the composition of the larger circle from which public initiative should proceed, one of us, a man of passionate concentration and judicial power of love, raised the consideration that too many Jews had been nominated.'

In principle Buber agreed, but felt unhappy about the spirit in which the objection appeared to have been raised. ' Obstinate Jew that I am,' he continued, ' I protested against the protest. I no longer know how from that I came to speak of Jesus and to say that we Jews knew him from within, in a way that remains inaccessible to the peoples submissive to him. " In a way that remains inaccessible to you "—so I addressed the former clergyman. He stood up, I too stood up ; we looked into the heart of one another's eyes. " It is gone," he said, and before everyone we gave one another the kiss of brotherhood.'

The Professor's final comment on the incident has a special bearing on the theme of this chapter. ' The discussion of the situation between Christians and Jews,' he wrote, ' had been transformed into a bond between the Christian and the Jew. In this transformation dialogue was fulfilled. Opinions were gone ; in a bodily way the factual took place.'

It is very unlikely that this was the first group of Christians and Jews to be drawn together in our day and generation by the ' presentiment of catastrophe '. It was certainly not the last. Nor has the threat, or even the experience, of disaster provided the only reason for meeting. In the field of Biblical scholarship, and of the study of the origins and development of their respective faiths, Christians and Jews alike have come to know and respect each other as never before.

In other words, the ' dialogue ' which, in the experience recorded by Martin Buber, found its fulfilment in a moment of time, has begun and is continuing on a much larger scale in the present confrontation of Christians and Jews in the world situation. In that total situation there have been frequent instances of the fulfilment or partial fulfilment of dialogue in the relations between individuals. This Jew has met that Christian and there has been understanding between them. In the more general field of community relations, however, the dialogue is likely to continue for years, perhaps even generations, and in so doing to provide abundant opportunity for all kinds of co-operative activity.

Our purpose in this chapter is threefold. We shall first examine those factors in the present situation which not only provide the opportunity, and indeed the need, for co-operation, but also determine the form it should take. Secondly, we shall consider on what basis inter-religious co-operation is both practicable and proper. Finally we shall review progress already made in this field.

Though much of what follows is necessarily concerned with human situations and with organizational problems, it is the writer's profound belief that the dialogue between Judaism and Christianity, between the Church and the Synagogue, and, in particular situations, between Christians and Jews, has its origin in the mind and purpose of God. That purpose may express itself, sometimes through and sometimes in spite of, our own endeavours to organize better human relations. When and how the fulfilment will come we cannot tell. But come it surely will in that day of which the prophet dreamed, when ' the Lord shall be one and His name one in all the earth '.

## 1. FACTORS MAKING FOR CO-OPERATION

Of the many factors in the contemporary situation which make for co-operation between Christians and Jews three are of outstanding importance.

The first, and perhaps the least spectacular, may prove in the end to be the most important. It is the recognition by a now considerable body of both Jewish and Christian scholars of the inadequacy, and all too often the inaccuracy, of their respective estimates of each other's religious position. In this connection the work of such scholars as George Foot Moore, Travers Herford, Herbert Danby, Strack and Billerbeck, Israel Abrahams and Claude Montefiore, to mention only a few of the pioneers, has already done much in breaking down ignorance and prejudice and in promoting mutual respect and understanding, without which any form of effective co-operation is impossible.

The two other factors are, first, the menace of antisemitism and secondly the disintegrating influences of materialist and secular interpretations of life and history. These two tendencies are closely related as to both their causes and their effects. Each is symptomatic of deep-seated disorders in the life, whether of the individual who subscribes to its teachings or of the community that is moulded by them. Each constitutes a threat to the stability and well-being, in the last resort, of the whole human family.

That the existence of antisemitism anywhere is a danger to Jews everywhere is only too tragically obvious. ' We cannot forget,' it was said at Amsterdam (1948), ' that we meet in a land from which 110,000 Jews were taken to be murdered. Nor can we forget that we meet only five communities to keep pace with man's insatiable curiosity in so many fields of scientific investigation, and with the amazing and at the same time bewildering profusion of his discoveries. The consequent development of a ' conflict between religion and science ' and the subjection of both Jewish and Christian religious sources to the processes of literary and historical criticism have done much to undermine the influence of religious institutions, to widen the gulf between religion and life, and to encourage those tendencies towards secularism and materialism which, as we have already seen, today constitute a major challenge to Church and Synagogue alike.

We find ourselves therefore in a situation in which Christians and Jews, hampered in their mutual relations by the unhappy consequences of nearly two thousand years of misunderstanding between them, are together threatened by forces hostile to both alike. It is a situation which calls for something much more positive and constructive than mutual defence. Mere condemnation of the enemy can serve no useful purpose. If the forces which at present threaten the very foundations of our civilization are to be defeated it can only be by the opposition of ' a more excellent way ', by the positive reaffirmation, not in words alone but in the life both of individuals and of communities, of those fundamental truths about the nature of God and man which, for all the differences that exist between Christians and Jews, are in fact part of their common inheritance.

To that end the urgent need for a greater degree of mutual understanding between Jews and Christians is obvious. Moreover, if there is to be effective co-operation between them it must be religiously inspired. At the same time, if further confusion is to be avoided, the limitations as well as the possibilities of such co-operation must be clearly seen and mutually accepted. The fact that they have many things in common must not be allowed to obscure the fact that there are also fundamental differences between Judaism and Christianity.

## 2. THE BASIS OF CO-OPERATION

The limitations are imposed partly by the mutual suspicions and fears which have for so long bedevilled the relations between Jews and Christians, and partly by the differences between them in matters of religious faith and practice.

There are Jews who appear instinctively to suspect any approach from the Christian side, even the friendliest, as merely a veiled form of evangelism or proselytization. There are Christians who fear that any talk of co-operation with Jews must necessarily compromise what they regard as a fundamental obligation to preach the gospel to Jews no less than to other people.

Both fears are understandable. Few stories of evangelistic endeavour reflect less credit on the Christian Church than some aspects of the traditional Christian approach to the Jew, of which the late Canon Lukyn Williams once wrote : ' It is only rarely that Christian writers have regarded Jews otherwise than from a level presupposed to be immeasurably higher than the Jewish, and have been able to keep out of sight their conviction that the unbelief of the Jews was due to sheer obstinacy. Christian writers have often lacked the knowledge, and too often even the love, that would have made their zeal effective.'[1]

On the other hand, nothing could be more unfortunate at the present time than any attempt to water down the distinctive witness either of the Christian or of the Jew to the faith that is in him. Man's need today is for a strengthening, not a weakening, of religious emphases.

When, soon after the setting up of a Council of Christians and Jews in London in 1942, such fears were expressed on both sides, the late Dr William Temple, who as Archbishop of Canterbury had played an important part in bringing the Council into being, wrote a letter to the late Chief Rabbi (Dr J. H. Hertz) in which he said :

> My own approach to this matter is governed by the consideration that the effectiveness of any religious

[1] *Adversus Judæos* (Cambridge University Press), p. 385.

ethical conduct in man's response to God as He makes Himself known in His wisdom and goodness '. Man is conceived as having been created by the will of God as ' both an individual and a member of society ' so that there can be ' true community only where there is full personal life and vice versa '. It is, therefore, ' the duty of men to respect in others the right to life, liberty, and personal dignity ', since ' each individual possesses worth as a person and must therefore treat others as such, while other persons and the community must accord similar treatment to him '. This principle involves ' recognition of his status as a member of society with a contribution to make to the whole, and is opposed to discrimination on grounds of colour, race, or creed '.

Acceptance of these principles in turn implies repudiation both of ' the individualism which would make man a law unto himself, and of the totalitarianism which would subordinate and sacrifice all other values to race, nation, state, class, or party '. It implies also recognition of two further complementary principles : first, that ' things must be subordinated to persons, and property rights made secondary to considerations of human welfare and social justice ' ; and secondly, that since ' nature is a revelation of God and a sphere of His purpose ' it is ' to be respected and not exploited '.

Then follows a point of very great importance. It is that the right attitude, whether of the community to persons, of persons to persons, or persons to things, ' cannot be fully achieved without the recognition, alike by the individual and the community, of God and of the relation of man and nature to Him ', a recognition which includes ' all that comes within the compass of worship '.

This joint affirmation of the value of public worship and of ' the need to participate in it if a right human order is to be achieved ' is of great importance in relation to any policy of co-operation in social service or educational activity. It follows, naturally, that ' religious communities have the right to exist and also the right to their own freedom of activity ', a right that must be recognized, for

without it ' the political community is impoverished '.
It must not be interpreted, however, as a sanction for
joint acts of worship, which, except in the most unusual
circumstances, may be open to serious misunderstanding.

Other points emphasized by the statement include respect
for the family, the obligation upon Governments to recognize
' the social, political, and religious rights and responsibilities
of individuals and groups ', and the obligation upon society
itself ' to use all its resources for the welfare of all its members '.    The whole leads to the conclusion that ' man's
recognition of himself and of his neighbour as children of
God should issue in a charity and righteousness which,
while but imperfectly embodied in the forms and laws of
organized society, work constantly to transform them into
an ever more adequate expression '.[1]

While there is little, if anything, in the statement that
is new to either, the recognition by both Christians and
Jews alike that it represents the common ground of religious
faith and ideals on the basis of which they can in fact
co-operate makes it a document of outstanding significance.


3. ADVENTURES IN CO-OPERATION

The beginnings of organized co-operation between
Christians and Jews in the present century go back to the
year 1923, when the Federal Council of Churches of Christ
in America set up a Committee on Good Will between
Jews and Christians.    This step was occasioned by the
growing influence of the Ku Klux Klan.    The Klan, with
its slogan ' America for the Americans ', was a product of
the economic depression that followed the first World War.
It was an outstanding example of the type of ' hate movement ' which, as in the case of the Nazis in Germany,
thrives on the exploitation for its own ends of deep-seated
racial and religious prejudices.    Jews, Roman Catholics,
Negroes, and all ' foreigners ' became alike the objects of

[1] The full text of this statement, with certain papers written in preparation for it, is published by the Council of Christians and Jews in the
pamphlet *The Foundations of Our Civilization*.

its propaganda and the victims of its attacks. But, as the leaders of the Federal Council of Churches quickly realized, it was the nation as a whole, and not merely the members of its minority groups, that was threatened. They recognized, too, that a more comprehensive body was needed than the Committee on Good Will between Christians and Jews.

Accordingly, in 1928, a National Conference of Christians and Jews was launched as a joint organization of 'Protestants, Catholics, and Jews'. Its basis, as defined by its by-laws, was belief ' in a spiritual interpretation of the universe'. Its purpose was :

> To promote justice, amity, understanding, and co-operation among Protestants, Catholics, and Jews, and to analyse, moderate, and finally eliminate inter-group prejudices which disfigure and distort religious, business, social, and political relations, with a view to the establishment of a social order in which the religious ideals of brotherhood and justice shall become the standards of human relationships.

The programme of the National Conference has been from the outset, in the broadest sense of the term, educational. It has included speaking tours by teams comprising a Protestant minister, a Roman Catholic priest, and a Jewish rabbi ; conferences on human relations at both the national and local level ; research projects into the causes of prejudice and inter-group tension and ways of dealing with them ; the organization (since 1934) of an annual observance of ' Brotherhood Week ' during the week of Washington's birthday ; the publication and syndication of Religious News Service ; the production of literature and visual aids ; and many other ancillary activities that inevitably go with such a programme.

The leaders of the organization itself would be the first to acknowledge the difficulty of assessing the results of their activities, though statistics with regard to the size of their staff, the number of their supporters, and their budget (now somewhere in the region of two million dollars) are impressive. That they have encountered many difficulties is reflected, by implication at least, in a statement of policy adopted by the Executive Committee of the Board of Directors of the Conference in 1949, where it is stated, for example, that the National Conference of Christians and Jews seeks to promote the brotherhood of man ' not on a secularist basis, but explicitly on the religious basis of the fatherhood of God '.   It ' strives for brotherhood in those ways which are acceptable to Protestants, to Catholics, and to Jews . . . not on the basis of removing religious differ- ences, or by accepting some non-theistic faith such as the so-called " religion of democracy ", or by declaring that one religion is as good as another '.   The charge of religious indifferentism, implied by the concluding phrase of this sentence, is still further refuted by the statement that the National Conference :  ' acknowledges the freedom of the Catholic or the Jew or the Protestant to hold that his faith is the one true faith.   It does not affirm such a holding by any one of the three, for it could obviously do so only at the expense of the other two ;  but neither does it disaffirm. It is not indifferentist, therefore.   It is simply, as it must be, non-preferential.'

On the question of joint worship, the statement declares that the National Conference ' does not sponsor joint worship, exchange of pulpit, or common observance of Christian and Jewish holy days.   Nor does it disapprove such practices on the part of those who in good conscience participate in them.'   It is not, in fact, ' an " inter-faith " organization, in the sense in which that word is commonly understood ', but rather a ' civic agency . . .' which ' seeks to promote affirmative co-operative action among Protes- tants, Catholics, and Jews in areas of common civic concern '.

In Great Britain the story goes back to the year 1924, when the Social Service Committee of the Liberal Jewish Synagogue, feeling that ' in spite of serious differences of belief, Jews and Christians were at one in their desire to bring nearer the Kingdom of God on earth ', consulted a number of other religious bodies, set up an organizing committee, and convened a Conference with the stated object of affording ' an opportunity to Jews and Christians

9

to confer together on the basis of their common ideals and with mutual respect for differences in belief'. This Conference, which took place in November 1924, had as its theme ' Religion as an Educational Force'. It aroused so much interest that what had previously been an *ad hoc* Committee was given a more permanent status. Eventually, in 1927, a Society of Jews and Christians was formally established ' to promote fellowship and understanding between Jews and Christians '.

Further Conferences were held and lectures on matters of common religious interest delivered by distinguished scholars on both sides. In the orthodox circles, however, both Jewish and Christian (but especially Jewish) these activities were viewed with a certain suspicion as tending towards religious indifferentism. When, therefore, some years later, the growth of antisemitism gave rise to grave anxiety on the part of Christians as well as Jews in Great Britain, and the need for co-operative action in opposition to this evil became clear, it was found impracticable, in view of the earlier criticisms of the Society, to expand it into a national organization of the kind required by this new situation.

In the meantime, however, a great deal of active co-operation between Jews and Christians had developed in work for refugees from Nazi persecution. This practical experience of co-operation in human service, and the relationships of mutual understanding and goodwill that resulted from it, provided a basis for the setting up in March 1942 of a Council of Christians and Jews whose Joint Presidents were the Archbishop of Canterbury, Cardinal Hinsley, the Moderator of the Church of Scotland, the Moderator of the Free Church Federal Council, and the Chief Rabbi. The aims of this new body were : ' To check and combat all forms of religious and racial intolerance ; to promote mutual understanding and goodwill between Christians and Jews in all sections of the community ; to promote fellowship between Christian and Jewish youth organizations in educational and cultural activities ; and to foster co-operation between Christians and Jews in social and community service.'

A significant feature of this statement of aims, especially in view of its origin, is the absence of any reference to antisemitism. The omission, however, was not accidental, for those who were responsible for setting up the Council took the view that antisemitism is only one of the many forms of racial and religious intolerance which threaten mankind, that it is symptomatic of deeper disorders, and that it is to the remedying of these underlying evils that Christians and Jews in particular should address themselves.

As in the case of the American Conference of Christians and Jews, the work of the Council in Great Britain has developed along broadly educational lines. It has been directed partly to the promotion of mutual understanding between members of the two faiths, and partly to interesting them in matters of common concern and civic responsibility in both national and international affairs, including problems of religious liberty, of race relations, and also, for example, Middle East affairs.

The methods employed by the Council are, save for certain differences of accent and idiom, similar to those employed by the American organization, and indeed by all bodies concerned with educational work. The name of its bi-monthly magazine, *Common Ground*, is in itself a reflection of the purpose running through all the Council's activities.

Another body already in existence some years before the outbreak of the second World War was the South African Society of Jews and Christians. Of quite independent origin, this Society began in 1939 to publish a monthly magazine entitled *Common Sense* which, though designed primarily ' to combat antisemitism and to foster better understanding and goodwill between the Jewish community and its Christian neighbours ', had also a wider purpose. As in the case of both the American and the British organizations, the founders of the South African Society believed that one form of prejudice could not be isolated from other manifestations of irrational thinking and group antagonisms or from the deep-seated economic and social problems of our society. *Common Sense* therefore developed into a journal devoted to ' the combating of all forms of racial and group prejudice, the promotion of inter-faith and inter-cultural education, and the fostering of constructive thinking on South Africa's major problems '.

It is a melancholy reflection both on the urgent need for this kind of activity and on the difficulties of sustaining it that the work of this Society came to be concentrated more and more into this one channel of the publication of a magazine, and that even this exceedingly healthy and challenging organ for stimulating public opinion was compelled to cease publication.

Two other examples of joint organizations within the British Commonwealth are the Canadian Council of Christians and Jews and the New South Wales Council of Christians and Jews in Sydney, Australia. The former, which was originally set up shortly before the second World War, owed much to the initiative and persistence of Dr Edwin Silcox, who, in 1934, had published a study of relationships in the United States and Canada under the title *Catholics, Jews, and Protestants* which is still perhaps the most comprehensive survey so far undertaken in this particular field. The Canadian Council itself virtually ceased to function in the immediately post-war period, largely on account of differences of opinion among some of its leading members with regard to Zionism and the changing political situation in the Middle East. It was revived, however, in 1947, with the appointment of a new director. Its statement of purpose is identical with that of the National Conference of Christians and Jews in the United States, and its programme is very similar to that of the larger body.

The New South Wales Council came into being chiefly as a protest against the Nazi persecution of Jews and was broadly sympathetic to the Zionist claim that Palestine offered the only real solution of the problem. There does not appear to have been any considerable programme of local activities, and the Council was allowed to lapse after the State of Israel had been established. There is evidence, however, of continuing interest in the question of Jewish-Christian co-operation in Australia, and it seems probable that some new attempts may be made to launch a joint body.

In Europe a Study Conference of Swiss Christians and Jews took place at Walzenhausen, near Zürich, in November 1945. A Declaration published by this Conference laid great stress on the need for ' unprejudiced teaching concerning the origins of Christianity ', for the education of Christians and Jews ' from their very childhood in a spirit of mutual respect and mutual understanding ', and for governmental action in the fight against all forms of religious and racial hatred. The statement urged that work of this kind should be undertaken partly by separate Jewish and Christian groups and partly through united action. The practical outcome of the Conference was the setting up of the ' Christlich-jüdische Arbeitsgemeinschaft zur Bekämpfung des Antisemitismus in der Schweiz ', which later shortened its title by omitting the words ' zur Bekämpfung des Antisemitismus '.

These, then, were the bodies specifically concerned with problems of Jewish-Christian relations that were already in being when, at the joint invitation of the National Conference of Christians and Jews and the British Council of Christians and Jews, an International Conference took place at Oxford in August 1946.

This Conference, in addition to producing the statement on the fundamental postulates of Judaism and Christianity, gave particular attention to the general problem of group tensions with special reference : to antisemitism ; to religious liberty ; to the claims of justice in social, economic, and political life ; and to the need for education and training for citizenship.

Of particular relevance to our present discussion were certain findings of the Commission on Religious Freedom, which, it was agreed, ' should include at least :

(a) freedom from compulsion to do what one's conscience forbids ;

(b) freedom to worship according to conscience and to maintain distinctive religious observances ;

(c) freedom to preach, teach, educate, and persuade '.

In connection with the third of these points the Conference laid particular emphasis on the freedom of parents to have their children brought up in their own faith, and also on the fact that ' displaced or orphaned children should normally be restored to the community to which they originally belonged and which claims them, unless, being of mature age, they have made their own free choice of religion ; but ', the report added, ' varying conditions affecting the welfare of such children make it difficult to frame a rule applicable to every single case '.

On the question of evangelism and missionary activities, which were considered under the general heading of ' freedom to persuade ', it was agreed that ' religious convictions can be attained only in freedom and not as the result of compulsion or improper inducement.  Freedom to persuade should be limited to direct advocacy, and should in no case be accompanied by any form of economic or social pressure '.  This statement, as in the case of all other statements issued by this particular Conference, carried the consent of Roman Catholic, Protestant, and Jewish participants.

A practical outcome of the Conference was an attempt to set up a permanent international organization of Christians and Jews.  Two further international Conferences of Christians and Jews were held at Seelisberg in 1947 and Fribourg in 1948.  The 1947 Conference was devoted to discussion of the problem of antisemitism in Europe. Particular attention was given to the task of the Churches in relation to antisemitism and the report of the Commission which dealt with this problem attracted widespread interest and attention.  Familiarly known as the ' Ten Points of Seelisberg ', the report might well be regarded as an anticipatory expansion of the Amsterdam statement that ' the Churches in the past have helped to foster an image of the Jews as the sole enemies of Christ, which has contri-buted to antisemitism in the secular world '.  The Seelisberg Conference, addressing itself to the Churches, expressed ' the firm hope that they will be concerned to show to their members how to prevent any animosity towards the Jews which might arise from false, inadequate, or mistaken presentations of the teaching and preaching of the Christian doctrine, and how on the other hand to promote brotherly-love towards the sorely-tried people of the old covenant '.

To this end it was suggested that such points as the following be emphasized in Christian teaching : ' that One God speaks to us all through the Old and the New Testaments ; that Jesus was born of a Jewish mother of the seed of David and of the people of Israel, and that His everlasting love and forgiveness embrace His own people and the whole world ; that the fundamental commandment of Christianity, to love God and one's neighbour, proclaimed already in the Old Testament and confirmed by Jesus, is binding upon both Christians and Jews in all human relationships without any exception '. It was also urged that care be taken ' to avoid distorting or misrepresenting biblical or post-biblical Judaism with the object of extolling Christianity ', and also, to quote only one more of the ten points, ' to avoid presenting the Passion in such a way as to bring the odium of the killing of Jesus upon all Jews or upon Jews alone. It was ', the statement adds, ' only a section of the Jews in Jerusalem who demanded the death of Jesus, and the Christian message has always been that it was the sins of mankind which were exemplified by those Jews, and the sins in which all men share that brought Christ to the Cross.'

Glimpses of the obvious though these may be to many, they are far from being self-evident to all Christians, and there can be little doubt that greater attention on the part of preachers and teachers to matters of historical fact and perspective as well as to a more appreciative and sympathetic presentation of the Jewish background of the Christian gospel would help very considerably in disposing of some of the traditional stereotypes of ' the Jew ' still widely current in Christian circles. For their part, the Jewish members of the Conference which produced this report declared their intention of seeking to avoid in Jewish teaching anything which might prejudice good relations between Jews and their Christian neighbours. Awareness on both sides of the importance of such matters as these is growing as a result of increasing contact between Jews and Christians and is bound to contribute to the general amelioration of their mutual relations.

During the period immediately following the Oxford Conference of 1946 a number of joint groups were set up in France (where the Amitié Judéo-Chrétienne still functions in Paris though on a relatively small scale), in Italy, and particularly, through the initiative of the National Conference of Christians and Jews, in the American Zone of Germany, where Councils of Christians and Jews began to operate in a number of leading cities. Towards the end of 1948, however, some of the American leaders, feeling that a Jewish-Christian basis of co-operation was not sufficiently wide for what they envisaged as a world task of promoting the spirit and practice of brotherhood, withdrew from the attempt to build up an international Council of Christians and Jews, and in the summer of 1950 launched a new organization to be known as ' World Brotherhood '. Some of their former colleagues were left wondering whether the purpose of this new movement to promote on a world scale ' justice, amity, and understanding and co-operation among people varying as to religion, race, nation, or culture ', though unexceptionable as an ultimate ideal, was not in fact too comprehensive to be effectively practicable at the present time. Nor did its basis of membership as being open to ' all who believe in a spiritual interpretation of the universe and who derive their inspiration therefrom ' seem to offer quite such a positive platform of co-operative endeavour as, for example, the Oxford statement on the fundamental postulates of Judaism and Christianity. For the time being, therefore, such international contacts as exist in the specific field of organized Jewish-Christian co-operation are of an informal and unofficial character.

There are, however, other areas in which co-operation between Christians and Jews has developed in response to some particular need. There is also one important area in which, though the issue of co-operation as such does not arise, attitudes have been considerably influenced by a growing recognition of its importance.   This is the field of missionary work.

Reference has already been made to the attitude of the Jewish members of the British Council of Christians and Jews on this matter (see page 124), and also to the discussion at Oxford in 1946 of what is involved in the right to persuade.   It is particularly interesting, however, to see how considerations of this kind have been increasingly reflected during recent years in discussions of missionary method and policy.   This tendency was already apparent in the reports of the Budapest-Warsaw Conferences on the Christian Approach to the Jew in 1927 and of a further Conference held at Atlantic City in 1931.   It was specifically emphasized in the recommendations of the Commission on the Christian approach to the Jews at Amsterdam in 1948 that the member Churches of the World Council of Churches should ' seek to recover the universality of Our Lord's commission by including the Jewish people in their evangelistic work '.   The Assembly also recommended, first, that the Churches should ' encourage their people to seek for brotherly contact with and understanding of their Jewish neighbours, and co-operation in agencies combating misunderstanding and prejudice ', and further, ' that in mission work among Jews they should scrupulously avoid all unworthy pressures or inducements '.   These same points were further emphasized in a leaflet entitled *The Jew in the Parish* published and widely distributed by the British Council of Churches in December 1950.

Although such declarations are unlikely to make the Christian missionary enterprise more acceptable to Jews, it is at least reasonable to hope that they may help to remove that almost unconscious attitude of assumed superiority on the part of the Christian which has for so long hampered the development of normal relations with his Jewish neighbours.

Three other significant examples of Jewish-Christian co-operation are, first, the work of the special department of the Ministry of Religious Affairs in Israel which is responsible for relations with the Christian Churches and religious institutions ; secondly, the work of the so-called Churches Groups of the National and London Councils of Social Service in the United Kingdom ; and finally the work of a body, also in Great Britain, known as the Religious Bodies Joint Consultative Committee.

No Christian visitor to Israel can fail to be impressed with the pains taken by the Ministry of Religious Affairs to ensure the maintenance and development of friendly and co-operative relations with the many and varied Christian institutions and Churches still operating in that country. A bulletin entitled *Christian News from Israel*, published by the Ministry, serves not only as a channel of information on matters of general Christian interest, but also as a medium for the publication of articles by Christian writers and scholars. It is interesting, for example, to recall that on the Eve of the Christmas Festival the President of a Jewish State should issue a message of ' heartfelt greetings and good wishes to our Christian fellow-citizens and to Christian visitors and sojourners in this country '. President Ben Zvi (this was in December 1952) went on to express the hope that they would ' all enjoy a Merry Christmas ' and ' that the New Year now being ushered in may see the further development of goodwill and friendship between all sections of our population '.

In the second area, that of co-operation in social service, it is a characteristic feature of the period in which we are living that initiative in the fields of education, health, and the social services should pass from the religious to the civic authorities. There is much to be said in favour of such a development, always providing that those responsible for civic administration do not forget the underlying religious motives which inspired the pioneer work of their predecessors ; and that religious leaders resist any temptation to leave the initiative entirely with the ' powers that be '.

It was to guard against just such dangers that the National and London Councils of Social Service some few years ago set up what have come to be known as ' Churches Groups ', whose membership is drawn from the Jewish as well as from the Anglican, Roman Catholic, and Free Church

CHRISTIAN AND JEWISH CO-OPERATION 139

sections of the community. Consultative rather than executive in their function, the Churches Groups have made careful studies of a wide range of social problems from the religious point of view. Recent examples of such activities are the holding of a conference of representative religious leaders, administrators, and social workers to consider the provision of churches and community centres in new housing areas, and the publication of a handbook for social workers on the moral principles which should underlie their work.

The Religious Bodies Consultative Committee (a not very exciting name for what is a really significant group) was set up shortly after the end of the second World War to serve as a link between the Churches and the Jewish community on the one hand and the United Nations Association on the other. Its members are appointed by the Anglican and Free Churches through the British Council of Churches, and also by the Roman Catholic and Jewish authorities. Its purpose is ' to promote consultation and co-operation in the field of international affairs '. Statements published by this body dealing with the Spiritual Inheritance of Europe and the Moral Foundations of International Law aroused considerable interest in the denominational press in Great Britain and in religious circles both in this country and abroad.

Another important example of co-operation in the field of international affairs is the work of the United States Committee for a United Nations Genocide Convention. This Committee, which was set up in 1948, was strongly representative of the Roman Catholic, Protestant, and Jewish communities in the United States. Its activities, however, were by no means restricted to one country. In September 1948 the Committee filed with the General Assembly of the United Nations petitions gathered from 166 organizations in 28 different countries and claiming to represent more than two hundred million people, and there can be little doubt that this work in what was obviously a very natural and proper field for Jewish-Christian co-operation helped materially in securing the adoption of the

Genocide Convention by the United Nations General Assembly on 9th December of that year.

CONCLUSION

Three things remain to be said by way of general observation. That the survey of areas of co-operation is far from exhaustive will long since have become patently obvious to the reader, and apologies are due to many whose activities in this field have been either inadequately treated or, still worse, ignored altogether. But if the examples are few, they are at least typical and have some bearing on what was said earlier about the need and opportunity for co-operation. Some readers may feel too much attention has been given to general statements and not enough has been said about methods and techniques. But this lack of balance, if such indeed it is, has been intentional. Nothing is easier in this technological age than to make suggestions as to ways and means of doing things. What is much more important, but all too often taken for granted, is the reason for doing them. There are many who are 'all for co-operation' and too few who have really considered why, and to what end !

Secondly, and closely related to the preceding point, is the importance of recognizing that co-operation is not an end in itself. Neither are such ideals as those of tolerance, mutual respect, goodwill, or even brotherhood, the ultimate goals of human existence. At least they cannot be so regarded by either Christians or Jews for whom the real end of all living is to know God and to enjoy Him for ever. The first and the great commandment is for both alike the essentially personal and individual one : ' Thou shalt love the Lord thy God with all thy heart, with all thy mind, and with all thy strength '. The second, it is true, is ' like unto it ', but is in the last analysis meaningless apart from the first. In so far, therefore, as many of the motives and ideals to which such frequent reference has been made in this chapter can be made to serve that supreme end, well ! If not that, then co-operation between Christians and

Jews or between Christians and anyone else may well prove to be of little avail in averting the disasters which today threaten all mankind. But in the meantime there is urgent need for serious thought on the part of Jews and Christians alike as to what we mean when we use such words as tolerance, mutual understanding, and goodwill.

Finally, and perhaps most important of all, we return to the point from which we set out, the fact of the dialogue. We spoke at the beginning of the dialogue between Church and Synagogue, the dialogue which has continued through the centuries between the Christian and the Jew, neither of whom has ever really been able to forget, to escape from, or to dispense with the other. In the last analysis, however, we are concerned with a dialogue not between man and man, but between man, whether he be Christian or Jew, and God.

In that dialogue the first word is with God. Neither Judaism nor Christianity knows anything of God as a remote, abstract, and impersonal first cause. Creator He most certainly is ; but according to the faith both of the Christian and of the Jew, the act of creation itself is in its very essence an act of communion. Both, though with differing emphases, can subscribe to the affirmation that it was by ' the Word which was in the beginning with God that all things were created '. For both it is an axiom of their faith that this same God spoke unto the fathers in the prophets by divers portions and in divers manners ; for the Christian no less than for the Jew He is ' the God of Abraham, of Isaac, and of Jacob '.

Man's part in the dialogue, however, has been fumbling and faltering to a degree. It still is. Having heard part, we are all too ready to assume that we have heard the whole, and to affirm that our own particular interpretation of what we have heard must necessarily be the right one. Neither Church nor Synagogue has had any monopoly in the matter of bigotry, or of intolerance. Too often the dialogue between them has developed into an argument, which for both has drowned the Living Word of God Himself.

But if the first Word was with God, so also is the last.

The Christian affirms what the Jew cannot yet accept, that the Word became flesh and dwelt among us. But if at that point there is what seems to be an insurmountable barrier between them, it may be well for the Christian to reflect on the challenge of Martin Buber's word to the clergyman who protested that too many Jews had been nominated to share in a venture of Christian-Jewish co-operation in the face of an imminent disaster. 'We Jews', said the Professor, 'know him from within in a way that remains inaccessible to the peoples submissive to him.'

The end is not yet, but it is not unreasonable to hope that every act of co-operation, every experience of meeting, every means of communication, which helps in the breaking down of age-long barriers of prejudice and misunderstanding between Christians and Jews may serve not only to further the dialogue but also to hasten the coming of the Kingdom of God.

# VIII

# THE CHURCH AND THE HEBREW CHRISTIAN

## H. L. ELLISON

EARLY in the century calculations were made by Jewish writers of the cost of a convert to Christianity for any of the Jewish missionary societies. As late as 1929 Israel Cohen estimated the cost for the London Jews' Society in 1894 as something between £600 and £3000 per head ; less careful and reputable calculations had put it as high as £10,000 a head, and this figure is still sometimes met with in Jewish circles. The main inference was not that the Church was pouring out money to buy Jewish souls, but rather that practically no Jews were being converted.

The widespread acceptance of such estimates among Jews need not surprise us. All minority groups defend themselves by an unconscious readiness to accept judgments which support and justify their peculiar position. It is, however, absurd that these estimates were widely accepted in some Christian circles, where they have not completely died out.

However absurd the Christian acceptance of such estimates may be, it is easy to understand. The vast majority of Christians consider that it is virtually a miracle if a Jew comes to faith in Christ, and that the Church's approach to the Jew is at best a magnificent gesture. When we tell them that *proportionately* the Church's proclamation to the Jew in the 19th and 20th centuries has been *at least* as successful as its proclamation in the average mission field, and indeed much more successful than in some, we are met with polite incredulity. Yet so far as the 19th century is concerned, the statement is substantiated by serious works

144 THE CHURCH AND THE JEWISH PEOPLE

of research, such as J. F. A. de la Roi : *Die evangelische Christenheit und die Juden* and D. A. Rosenthal : *Konvertiten-bilder aus dem neunzehnten Jahrhundert* ; no one familiar with the facts is likely to suggest that the flow of converts has grown smaller in the 20th century.

Through most unfortunate circumstances we are able to check the extent of the flow from the Synagogue to the Church in at least one country. It was probably only those actually involved in relief and rescue work among the victims of Hitler's racial policy who fully realized how many Christian ' Volljuden ' (full Jews) there were among them. Though the number of ' Mischlinge ersten und zweiten Grades ' (half and quarter Jews) was greatly exaggerated by some, it is clear that the number of known cases—many, especially ' Mischlinge zweiten Grades ', never had their origin discovered—was far greater than Hitler and his advisers ever realized when they launched their all-out Jewish policy. There can be no doubt that Professor Dalman was saying no more than the literal truth when he said, ' If all the Jews who have embraced Christianity had remained a distinct people instead of being absorbed by the nations among whom they dwelt, their descendants would now be counted in millions '.

The disappearance in large measure of Hebrew Christian converts through their absorption by the Gentile surroundings in which they found themselves had a variety of causes, the most potent of which was normally the attitude of the Church itself. At most times it actively fostered this absorption, and virtually never hindered it. We may well ask ourselves what were the motives behind such an apparently foolish policy, which generation by generation condemned the Church to begin its witness to Israel anew without ever profiting from its successes in the past, and which led many of its own members to believe that the conversion of a Jew was a rarity.

We shall later see that some of the reasons for the Church's policy were inherent in the situation itself and could not have been avoided. In part, however, the Church's policy has been an unrealized inheritance from the Middle

Ages.  The Mediaeval Church's great vision of catholicity
led in turn to one of uniformity.  The attempt to achieve
this goal by the use of force gave its leaders quite under-
standably a guilty conscience.  The use of force to bring
men to Christ raised the suspicion that every deviation
from orthodox practice, every retention of the past, gave
evidence of a merely half-hearted acceptance of the new.
It became a spiritual necessity to cut every link that could
bind the convert to his past.  Inasmuch as in Orthodox
Judaism religion enters into every detail of life, it meant
that the convert was expected to change all the externals
of life as well.  The Reformation churches took over this
tradition without much analysis of the motives behind it.

There was, however, an even deeper reason.  Today
almost every Reformed theologian regrets the undue
influence of Greek thought in Christian theology and desires
that the Hebrew element should have its due place once
more.  But for the early Gentile churches the Synagogue
was a feared and little understood enemy, and the Judaizer
was regarded as the subtlest and most dangerous enemy of
the Christian Church.  This phobia has persisted down the
centuries, and it is only comparatively recently that a few
have come to realize that the convert's wish to preserve
some of the spiritual riches of the Synagogue in his new
faith did not mean that he was trying to re-establish a
legalistic Christianity.  In other words, while the Church
preached Jesus to the Jew as the completion of the Old
Testament, it has too often also presented Him as the
complete negation of the Synagogue.

As a result of these two tendencies the Church has for the
most part been precluded from even considering the
possibility of the continuance of the Hebrew Christian as
a separate and discernible element within the Church
universal.  So far from lamenting his complete assimilation,
it has greeted it as something entirely desirable.

The pressure of the Church has been powerfully reinforced
by strong tendencies on the Jewish side.

Far more than the average Jew realizes, Jewry has been
preserved over the centuries not only by his religion but

10

also by that social discrimination exercised by both Christian and Moslem which found its extremest expression in the ghetto. Much that popular opinion labels Jewish has little or no relationship either with Judaism or with the Jews' remote oriental ancestry—the discovery of the oriental Jew has been a major shock for many of the pioneer founders of the new State of Israel. It has sprung rather from the artificial and often abnormal life of the ghetto.

In Western and Central Europe the ghetto vanished at the end of the 18th century or during the course of the 19th, as a result of that humanistic liberalism which reached its climax in the French Revolution ; in America it never existed. But when the ghetto vanished, unless indeed it was artificially preserved by the Synagogue, very much that was looked on as intrinsically Jewish gradually vanished too, and the Jew was revealed as being much more like his Gentile neighbours than had been imagined for centuries. Today Jewry has reacted against the whole-hearted assimil-ation of last century. But it is all too often overlooked that while in this assimilation much was voluntary and inten-tional, even more was the violent but necessary return to an equilibrium once the artificial barriers of the ghetto had been removed. Quite apart from that, though, much of the modern criticism is unfair. The transformation in the Jew's lot was so violent and sudden, 19th century humanism so alluring and dazzling, that no Jew should be blamed if he failed clearly to see the boundary between the incidental and essential in his heritage, and as a result so often threw that which was precious and vital overboard together with that which was best lost, or if he was some-times unduly ready to accept the opinions of his age about his ancestral religion.

If the pull of assimilation proved so strong for the Jew, it hardly needs to be pointed out that it was bound to be even stronger in the case of the average Hebrew Christian. In his case the expectation of the Church and the pull of the spirit of the age were powerfully reinforced by the attitude of Jewry itself, which refused to recognize that the ' apostate ' had any part or lot in the heritage of his people. To become a Christian was looked on as the one act which, except in the rarest cases, infallibly cut off the convert from his people. It has only been in recent decades that the purely political Zionist has been prepared to consider recognizing the Hebrew Christian as a Jew.

The reintegration of the Jew into modern society meant his rediscovery of Christianity ; the form of Christianity he most commonly met was the emasculated humanistic Christianity of last century, with its rationalism and depreciation of dogma. Obviously Christianity so presented created fewer intellectual obstacles for the average Jew. The charge so often made by Jew and Christian alike that so many of the ' conversions ' were merely for the sake of social convenience or advantage does little credit to those that make it. Anyone familiar with the conditions of last century knows full well that the vast majority of the converts stood spiritually no lower than their Gentile neighbours ; it was probably very rare for the ' conversion ' to involve intellectual dishonesty. We need hardly point out that such converts obviously took assimilation for granted.

We must not allow ourselves, however, to be deceived into thinking that these were the only converts of the period. There were many others, not men and women who had drifted into Christianity, but such as had been sought out by Christ's servants and been brought face to face with the living Christ. It is, however, striking that when we read their biographies we find that in the vast majority of cases an inner breach with the Synagogue had preceded their contact with Christians. So here too assimilation, though sometimes less rapid, was normally as certain as among those who had first drifted from Judaism before they drifted into Christianity. Indeed it was sometimes, out of gratitude to those who had won them for Christ, even more complete ; for they found in the Church that had become their spiritual home the deep-rooted and unquestioned expectation that they would assimilate.

The number during the 19th century who were converted while in the Synagogue and loving the Synagogue, and unaffected by the spirit of the new age, was small. Most were poor and humble people ; many lived in out-of-the-way places in East-Central and Eastern Europe, and were unknown even by name to all but a few particularly interested in missions to Jews. They found little understanding from their neighbours, whether Jewish or Christian, and even in many cases from the missionaries themselves. Most drifted to an unsatisfactory middle course : neither good Jews nor good Gentiles, not even fully-satisfied Christians, they left it to their children to solve the problem as best they might, which of course they normally did by assimilation. It is not surprising, then, that John Wilkinson, one of the outstanding English missionaries of the century and a man by no means friendly to the spirit of the age, should say *as a matter of course*, ' It is well known that the Church is bound in loyalty to her Lord to seek the conversion of the Jews, and it is equally well known that when the Jews become Christians they soon lose their nationality, and thus become incorporated with the Church '.[1] The naïvety of the view that where the Jew was concerned nationality was incompatible with Church membership should especially be noted. No contemporary missionary in any other field could have expressed himself thus.

The first signs of a real change of attitude towards the Hebrew Christian became obvious in the last quarter of the 19th century. This was mainly because certain outstanding converts, such as Joseph Rabinowitsch of Kisheneff, Rabbi Isaac Lichtenstein of Tapio-Szele, Christian Theodore Lucky in Galicia, Mark John Levy in Britain and the United States, forced themselves and their ' peculiar ' views on the attention of limited circles in the Christian Church.

With the approach of the present century a new spirit was abroad in Jewry. The Gentile West needed the catastrophe of 1914 to awaken it partially to the fact that the hopes of humanism were an empty dream. But the growth of political antisemitism in Germany from 1879, in Russia from 1881, and in Austria from 1882, and its open emergence in France in 1894 in the Dreyfus case, had

---

[1] *God's Plan for the Jew*, p. 57.

convinced the thinking Jew that he had little to hope for in the long run from assimilation.  He could not foresee the ghastly reality of Hitlerian antisemitism, with its concentration camps and gas chambers, but he had felt the cold blasts of insecurity warning him of worse to come.

Then, too, as Jewish emancipation went its way, its first intoxication and violence wore off, and it became possible to see the facts in truer perspective.  The union of traditional Judaism and modern scholarship had produced a line of outstanding scholars, some orthodox, some far from it, who were able to demonstrate that the Jew had his own rich contribution to make to the general wealth of mankind. And so a new pride began to grow up in being a Jew, though the term was winning new connotations it did not possess in the ghetto days.

This change in Jewish atmosphere gradually showed itself in the converts to Christianity.  It was a slow process, for the majority still came from the ranks of those to whom their share in common humanity meant more than their being Jews ; indeed, this is probably still true of the majority of converts in the United States today.

There is nothing accidental in the fact that the new trend first became clear in England.  It was traditionally the home of the eccentric, where within limits less conformity to accepted standards was demanded than elsewhere.  The triumph of Nonconformity had accustomed the bulk of the population to varieties of expression within the limits of Christian orthodoxy, and was gradually teaching them a new tolerance.  The typical pragmatic or common-sense philosophy of the Englishman kept him from troubling unduly about the possible implications of a movement and led him rather to judge it by the way it worked.  So when the Hebrew Christian Alliance was founded in 1866, there was, so far as we know, little opposition to it.  Nor was there, for that matter, when it extended to North America in 1915.  Similarly there was no opposition in English-speaking countries when the movement developed into the International Hebrew Christian Alliance in 1925.

At its foundation the Hebrew Christian Alliance was

vague as to its purpose. It conceived of itself mainly as providing a means by which Hebrew Christians could get to know one another better. This has always remained one of its main purposes. But at the foundation meeting the Rev. A. M. Meyer struck a note that has become increasingly important as the decades have passed : ' We cannot and will not forget the land of our fathers, and it is our desire to cherish feelings of patriotism '.[1] We do not know who first coined the term ' Hebrew Christian '—it is older than the Alliance—but its use showed spiritual genius ; it stressed that the Alliance was to be a union of persons who felt themselves peculiarly one by reason of a common national origin, not because of any peculiarity in their common faith. In most Continental languages such a term had been either unknown or unused, and the equivalent, ' Jewish Christian ', which came to be used instead raised among many theologians a strong but entirely unjustifiable suspicion that some form of Judaizing lay behind the movement.

The movement has retained its original quality of vagueness. The ' objects ' of the parent organization, now the Hebrew Christian Alliance of Great Britain, state merely : ' To unite Hebrew Christians in the bond of sympathy and prayer, to be a means of strength to one another, and a witness to their unbelieving brethren, as well as to the Church of Christ '. The ' aims ' of the International Alliance are of necessity more detailed, but do not really go beyond them in any important respect :

1. To foster a spirit of fellowship and co-operation among the Hebrew Christians throughout the world :
   (a) By the establishment of local National Alliances wherever possible ;
   (b) By watching over the spiritual development and general welfare of Hebrew Christians and encouraging them to be witnesses for Christ among Israel in every sphere of life, and thus set up again, under Divine guidance, ' the candlestick of witness within Jewry '.

[1] Quoted by Schonfield : *The History of Jewish Christianity*, p. 222.

2. To present a united witness on behalf of Christ not only to the Jewish people but to the World.

3. To interpret the spirit of the Jewish people to the Christian world, and the spirit of the Christian Gospel to the Jews.

4. To aid Churches and Societies in their selection of Hebrew Christian candidates offering themselves for the Ministry ; and supply them with information regarding converts as occasion may arise.

5. To identify Hebrew Christians with the Jewish people in the defence of their rights in countries in which these rights are denied them, and, when necessary, to protest against the spirit of antisemitism.

In other words, the Hebrew Christian Alliance has consistently stood for the principle that since Christianity is not bound to any nationality or national system, it is wrong to expect that converts from Judaism should *of necessity* identify themselves with and lose themselves in the nation among whom they live, though it has consistently and emphatically refused to condemn those that have done so. It has, however, also refused to identify itself with any of the various ideas of how the identity of the Hebrew Christian could and should be preserved, though it has been willing to act as a forum for their discussion.

As the Hebrew Christian concept began to spread at the end of last century in countries where Orthodox Judaism was still strong and Zionism was still in its infancy, it naturally led to the idea of Hebrew Christian religious communities, in which as much as possible of the heritage of the Synagogue should be preserved. Ready-made and obvious criticism should be checked by the thought that the only Christian communities normally available in these countries were the Roman Catholic or Eastern Orthodox, and that these were abhorrent to the Jews because of their use of images, their past history of persecution, and, at least in those lands, their actively antisemitic attitude. The only alternatives were normally either some small foreign Protestant group, in which the ethnic origin of its members was very strongly stressed, and rigid uniformity of outlook expected, or else some artificial creation of the missionary, by which he tried to transplant his home church, with doubtful success, to alien soil. So the idea of something specifically Hebrew Christian was superficially neither so absurd nor unnecessary as most supposed.

The conception received a powerful stimulus from the work of Joseph Rabinowitsch, who founded his Jewish Christian Synagogue in Kisheneff in 1885. Though his work became well known in Germany through his contacts with Franz Delitzsch, it has been all too little appreciated in English-speaking lands. While it was an obvious work of the Spirit, there was an element of the accidental about it. It seems clear that it was the use of the crucifix by both Lutherans and Russian Orthodox that was the deciding factor against his linking himself with either. So far as we can judge, his theology was entirely orthodox, and though he retained the observance of the Sabbath and the rite of circumcision, he made it absolutely clear that it was solely for national reasons. The movement was at first amazingly influential and far-reaching, but after Rabinowitsch's death in 1899 it rapidly disintegrated, to be finally swept away by the cataclysm of 1914. A work in Kisheneff between the two wars that claimed to be its continuation had in fact neither physical nor spiritual links with it.[1]

This failure after such a promising beginning deserves closer attention. Difficulties raised by the Tsarist government, the death of a great personality, and the fierce opposition of Jewry all played their part, but the real reason went deeper. Rabinowitsch had broken with strict Jewish orthodoxy long before he thought of Christ ; he was a fervent nationalist, and the bridge he was trying to build between the Church and the Synagogue was national rather than religious. At a time when in Jewry nationalism and orthodoxy were increasingly parting asunder, it needed more than his compromise to satisfy either the orthodox or the nationalists who found themselves being drawn to Christ. The religious problem latent in the existence of the Hebrew Christian and in the Church's approach to the Synagogue cannot be solved merely by the use of Hebrew

[1] For further details see Jocz : *The Jewish People and Jesus Christ*, p. 235.

in worship, or by the retention of certain religious customs to which a purely national character is ascribed.

We consider that C. T. Lucky, Mark John Levy, and P. P. Levertoff had, for all their failure, a truer conception of the issues involved. They saw that before the Church could speak to the heart of the Jewish people, it had to bring the message of Jesus the Messiah in the true Hebrew dress that it wore at the first. The two former were concerned mainly with the practical outworking of traditional Jewish life for the Hebrew Christian (and were as a consequence denounced as legalists by very many), the last in the moulding of worship in terms of the Synagogue tradition.

Rabinowitsch's practical work and the views put forward by these and other Hebrew Christians had striking reperecussions in certain limited Christian circles during the first fifteen years of the 20th century, particularly in the Church of England. It was widely recognized by them that the Church's approach to the Jew would inevitably result in the growth of Hebrew Christian congregations, which would tend in language and sometimes in practice to be separate from the other Christians of the land, though they would belong to one or other of the major world denominations. A few, especially Canon Box, went further and envisaged the emergence of a Hebrew Christian Church, which would take its place among the great national churches in the Church universal.

In contrast to the interest shown in some Christian circles, Jewry was virtually untouched by these proposals. We believe that this was in large measure because they came half a century or so too late. Though in the years before 1914 the orthodox Synagogue in Eastern Europe seemed unmoved and hardly influenced by modern thought, it was in fact on the point of collapse. It was in the position of the wooden house being devoured by termites : outwardly sound, it was ready to collapse once the storm came. Most orthodox Jews prepared to consider the possibility that there might be something not altogether bad in Christianity had already subconsciously begun to abandon the very positions that were being advocated by more extreme Hebrew Christian circles. After 1919 the centre of gravity in Jewry had definitely shifted from orthodoxy to Zionist nationalism, and so it hardly needs stressing that when such proposals were occasionally made in the inter-war period they raised little interest.

At a series of conferences between 1931 and 1937 the International Hebrew Christian Alliance discussed the question of a Hebrew Christian Church. At one stage the discussions were badly mismanaged and gave rise to serious misunderstandings of the Alliance's position, which are not entirely dead, even today. Finally, however, it became abundantly clear that neither in the circles represented by the Alliance, nor indeed in any responsible Hebrew Christian circles outside it, was there any genuine living desire for a Hebrew Christian Church. On the other hand there was almost universal recognition of the imperative need of Hebrew Christian communities, of which a number had already come into existence. Some of these were normal congregations in larger denominations marked out mainly by a predominantly Hebrew Christian membership ; others were independent churches in which the Jewish element was more marked, but in neither case was there in either theology or practice anything to suggest legalism or a revival of Ebionism.

In the course of these discussions it was easy to recognize five main reasons behind the wish to see Hebrew Christian communities established :

(a) Anti-Judaism and even antisemitism among Christians.

(b) The desire to avoid assimilation and to preserve national identity.

(c) The desire to create centres of Christian witness to Jewry.

(d) A deep longing for genuine Christian unity.

(e) A genuine and often well-founded dislike of much that is usual in Gentile churches.

The establishment of the State of Israel has radically changed the position. Unless the Church is to abandon its witness in that land there are bound to grow up in it an increasing number of Hebrew Christian churches, of which a number already exist. The forces abroad in Israel are certain to unite step by step the majority of these isolated churches into a unity, which though truly catholic will yet be distinct from other branches of the Church universal. Though it will not be exclusively Jewish, it will be in the truest sense Jewish and so, in some measure, a revival of the primitive Hebrew Christian Church. Let it be quite clear : we are not advocating anything, nor welcoming anything ; we are merely recognizing that a Hebrew Christian Church is as inevitable in Israel as, say, the South India Church was in India. What is more, historic circumstances over which we have had little control will prevent the churches of the West imposing their conceptions on it. We may delay or hasten its coming into being, but we cannot prevent it.

We are not concerned in this chapter with probable developments in Israel, nor do we think that when an indigenous Church of Israel is established it will have branches overseas. But its very existence would reinforce the already existing desire for Hebrew Christian communities, which has been reinforced as well by the tragic events in Jewry under Hitler. So the already mentioned motives should be considered more powerful than before and deserving of the closest study by all Christian leaders.

## ANTI-JUDAISM AND EVEN ANTISEMITISM AMONG CHRISTIANS

Anti-Judaism, the dislike of the Jew *on religious grounds*,[1] is one of the most widespread and deeply rooted Christian failings. In a nation-wide survey of the Lutheran churches of North America [2] 12.9 per cent of the nearly 7000 pastors contacted answered the questionnaire on the relationship of American Lutherans with the Jewish people. The answers were most illuminating, the more so when we realize that there would be a strong tendency throughout

[1] See my paper *Anti-Judaism* (Conference of Missionary Societies in Great Britain and Ireland).
[2] *The Lutheran Parish and the Jews*, in two Parts ; *An Analytical Study* and *A Survey* (The National Lutheran Council).

the country not to answer the questionnaire where there was active hostility.

Over the country as a whole only 6·9 per cent of the churches confessed to open antagonism, but only 37·7 per cent claimed to be definitely friendly ; we may well assume that in the remaining 55·4 per cent which were either indifferent or ' mixed ' the Hebrew Christian is likely to feel unwanted. We need not be surprised that the proportion of hostility rises among those churches that are in strongly Jewish areas ; what is serious is that the antagonism is up to the national average in areas where no Jews live ; and if we go by geographical areas, the antagonism is sometimes well above the average where no Jews are to be found. In other words, in many of the churches the dislike, active or passive, was due not to personal experiences but to traditional prejudice. Since such traditional prejudices are often unrealized, there can be little doubt that had the survey been carried out by trained observers instead of through a questionnaire a much higher percentage of dislike and antagonism would have been established. In addition it is generally these inherited dislikes that are hardest to eradicate, for they are normally irrational.

We have no comparable survey for other churches or lands, but fairly wide experience convinces us that it would be difficult anywhere over a representative area to obtain genuinely more favourable figures.

This should make us more ready to consider the complaints of Hebrew Christians. Converts from Judaism have generation after generation had the same complaints to make. When we have made all due allowances for undue subjectivity, there is too much residue and too much agreement in detail in widely separated lands, social classes, and denominations for the charges to be dismissed as mere hyper-sensitivity.

The worst complaint by Hebrew Christians is that they have been regarded with suspicion and their motives questioned ; in some circles it has been looked on as virtually axiomatic that behind their conversion was the spur of some material gain. Some, especially in liberal

circles, have looked on them as renegades, whose transfer
of religious allegiance has been considered deplorable.
Perhaps even more galling has been the contrast of those
good souls who have put them on a pedestal and regarded
them as a sort of circus curiosity. The worst hurt has
often been the slighting and critical way in which fellow
church-members have spoken in their presence of the Jews
and have taken it for granted that they fully agreed. More
easy to bear have been the overheard or reported remarks
about appearance, accent, and habits, though when the
convert has already been wounded and bruised they are
sometimes the last straw.

The one truly universal brotherhood, the one society
that really transcends all barriers of race, language, and
class, is the Church ; and if it does not do so, it is hardly
worthy of the name. But it is fatally easy in our great
urban centres for the local church and sometimes even the
denomination to be limited by race, culture, and class.
It is equally easy for the truly rural church to be dominated
by a limited homogeneous outlook. To both alike the
Hebrew Christian often comes as the main or even sole
challenge to inherited prejudices.

While we would do well to remember our Lord's warning
about those that cause one of His little ones to stumble,
there is, we believe, something even more important than
the spiritual comfort of the Hebrew Christians. Most of
them are, after all, reasonably resilient. They were
accustomed as Jews to hear slighting remarks, so after the
first bitter shock of hearing them in the Church they grow
cynically resigned. They learn not to expect too much
from their fellow-Christians and so they are spared dis-
appointment. Their children, if indeed they are not lost
to the Church altogether, grow up entirely assimilated, or
almost so. But the local church has done irreparable harm
to itself. By rejecting the practical lesson that Christ was
offering it, it has strengthened ancient prejudice and
narrowed its outlook even more, making itself even less
able to meet the problems of our changing world.

Active antisemitism the Church must condemn, especially

when it is found among its members, for it is always and everywhere evil, and there can never be any excuse for it. But it must also be willing to accept the discipline of the stranger within its gates, especially of the Hebrew Christian, who so often reveals to what extent it is controlled by the prejudices of the past instead of being governed by the mind of its Head.

We do well to remember that there was probably little active antisemitism in the churches of Germany in 1933, but anti-Judaism was rife. It was above all by exploiting this weakness that the Nazis were able to extend their influence over such a large section of the Church. We do well to weigh the considered opinion of many in the Confessional Church that the Christian's attitude to the Jews is a touchstone revealing the healthiness of the Church, and that a correct understanding of Rom. ix–xi is vital to a balanced Christian theology.

## The Desire to Avoid Assimilation and Preserve National Identity

Ever since nationality has come to the fore the Jew has occupied an equivocal position in European society and perhaps even more in that of the United States. In the days of religious intolerance it was easy enough to look on him as a foreigner, as a man of another race. With the growth of the secular state, with its wider tolerances, the memory of racial origin was expected to resolve itself in the wider loyalties of nationhood. In the second half of last century and the first decade of this it was assumed that this goal had largely been reached. Zionism was by many taken to be no more than the last flickers of an outgrown racialism soon to vanish among civilized men. Today we know that for good or evil nationalism is with us, and plays its part even in supra-national states.

Though we grant the Jew today every right to national existence, we still tend to feel that unless the Hebrew Christian lives in Israel there is something almost indecent in his maintaining his national identity. This is partly due to our never being quite certain whether Jew is a national or a religious term, but partly perhaps because more than we realize we tend with all our dislike of the Jew to expect a higher standard from him. In literature he has almost always been either the villain or the hero, a Shylock or a Nathan the Wise, but not just an ordinary member of society. Secretly we know that our national churches contradict the catholicity and unity of the Church of Christ, and so it comes as somewhat of a secret shock when we find the Hebrew Christian wanting to behave as he has seen us do.

At the enlarged meeting of the International Missionary Council's Committee on the Christian Approach to the Jews, in Basle, Switzerland, in 1947, no sectional report aroused more interest and careful study than that of the commission on the Church and the Hebrew Christian. But though it ran counter to the preconceived notions of many present, it was finally adopted almost unanimously. It reads:

> The people of Israel by virtue of their election by God have been and remain a mystery incapable of being fitted into the normal categories of national existence. It is impossible to explain their existence merely in terms of a religious community, and hence it is in no mere idealistic sense that we unanimously affirm that the Jew who by faith becomes a member of the Church of Christ in a very real sense remains a Jew, and may with full justification be called a Hebrew Christian.
>
> We affirm our conviction that it is normally every Christian's duty to ' abide in that calling wherein he was called ', and hence it should normally be expected that the Hebrew Christian will maintain his identity both in his relations with the Church and with his brethren according to the flesh. It should be considered legitimate and natural if this should lead to customs and theological language differing from that of his Gentile brethren. It is, however, certain that any such differences are primarily the result of human sin and frailty ; they do not imply that the Hebrew Christian has any privileged position in the Church, and they will assuredly vanish in the perfection of the eternal state.

We affirm that the manner in which the Hebrew Christian can best express and preserve his identity before his own people is one to which he must himself be led by the Holy Spirit. So long as the Hebrew Christian does not misrepresent thereby the teaching of Christ nor compromise with Judaism, the Gentile Christian should be prepared to show him all sympathy and understanding. We would, however, point out that the Hebrew Christian has a responsibility to his Gentile brother in the faith as well as to his brother according to the flesh, and that love should keep him from causing the former unnecessary misunderstanding and offence.

Convinced as we are that although national differences do not necessarily disappear in Christ national churches represent a departure from the mind of Christ for His Church, however much such a concession to human frailty may have been necessary, we would profoundly deplore the setting up of a Hebrew Christian Church, the more so as there seems to be no imperative reason for such an action.[1] We confess that the lack of love and understanding for the Hebrew Christians in many local churches is such that the setting up of local Hebrew Christian churches is unavoidable, but we would urge that no such step be ever taken unnecessarily, and that the existence of such a need should call the Church at large to penitence for its lack of love.

We recognize with grief that the Hebrew Christian all too often does not feel at home in the Church of Christ, and we call on the Church at large to realize that the main reasons are our lack of love which cannot find room for the stranger and the latent root of antisemitism which often poisons the Church's life where it is least realized. Attempts at unwarranted particularism on the part of the Hebrew Christian should rather be a ground for repentance for the Church than for condemnation of those who so often have had so little demonstration of the better way.

Unless the entirely unforeseeable happens, during the next few decades the vast majority of younger Jews outside

[1] The Committee met at a time before the present position in Israel could even be envisaged, and when there was neither the possibility of nor desire for such a Church in Palestine.

Israel are going to fall into three main groups. A minority will openly place Jewish-Israeli nationalism above the claims of the land of their birth. They will look on return to Israel as the goal of their lives ; and if by any means they are thwarted, they will look on the land of their sojourning as *galuth* (exile). The vast majority will seek to maintain an uneasy form of dual loyalty : in their emotions Israel will have the upper hand, in their intellects the land of their birth. Though their emotions will seldom be allowed to control their lives, Israel will effectively deny the possibility of assimilation. The third, and perhaps smallest, group will consist of those who though they remain loyal to the fact that they are Jews—however they may understand the term—will repudiate any but a sentimental and charitable interest in Israel.

One from this last group, though not quite so ready to assimilate as the emancipated Jew of last century, is not likely to present any particular problem to the Church, if he is won for Christ, unless indeed it be because he develops as a critic of popular Christian theology and practice. We deal with this side of the problem later.

The other two groups on the contrary will demand a major effort from the Church to re-think the presentation of its message. It has with the passage of time become relatively easy for the missionary to adapt himself to the economic, cultural, and nationalistic problems of the mission-field. Generations of missionary statesmen have taught the Church that much that is taken for granted in the Christianized lands of Western civilization should not and cannot be transplanted to Africa, the Far East, and the islands of the sea. But now the Church will be called on to apply the same principles at home, and it will not be easy.

Were the Church to preach in the State of Israel a gospel that involved those who accepted it in ceasing to be Jews nationally, its activities would very soon be banned. If it continues to preach such a gospel outside Israel to Jews, it may expect increasingly to be ignored by them. But the real test of the Church's sincerity and understanding will be in its attitude towards its converts. How they will decide they can best retain their national allegiance it is useless to speculate. Some will doubtless emigrate to Israel, but the majority will remain in the larger centres of Jewish population as a standing challenge to the Church's catholicity and understanding. Though organizations like the International Hebrew Christian Alliance through their national alliances will be able to do much to create mutual understanding, the main burden will perforce fall on local congregations.

## THE DESIRE TO CREATE CENTRES OF CHRISTIAN WITNESS TO JEWRY

Rather pathetically the Church has tended to take for granted that the convert from Judaism will perforce become a missionary to his own people. Some, like many of their Gentile friends, show no missionary zeal at all. Others, already detached from Judaism before their conversion, have been readier to turn to the Gentile with the Gospel. But there have always been individuals and groups with a burning desire to share their new-found faith with their own people.

They have seldom sought to replace the regular missionary work of the Church. They have rather sought to act as a bridge between the Church and the Jew, between the missionary and the Jew. To achieve this they have repeatedly in many lands tried to start groups and organizations in which the Jew would find himself at home and yet would be introduced to Jesus Christ. For a time many of them flourished and were sometimes remarkably successful, but they never, to our knowledge, lasted for long. The reason is not far to seek. While such efforts received the full support and sympathy of understanding missionaries, they very seldom had the blessing of the missionary's church. They could act as bridges to Christ, but not to the Church.

Nothing caused deeper dissatisfaction among Hebrew Christians in the period between the wars than the failure of the Church to understand and help their mediating efforts, and we may expect the dissatisfaction to increase in days to come.

The difficulty has been caused partly by the Church's traditional dread of Judaizing already referred to.  In all such mediating efforts it is obvious that as Jewish an atmosphere must be created as is consistent with loyalty to Christ.  In most cases for the convert it has no more than a sentimental or even utilitarian value, but the Gentile outsider has been all too ready to see in it the preparation for heresy.  Even more important is the fact that all too often the last span of the bridge was missing.  The Church's lack of interest or active distrust made it impossible to introduce the interested Jew to the Gentile Christian under the most favourable circumstances.  Unless at any rate some Gentile Church members are prepared to make the effort through such groups to learn the Jewish point of view and so meet the Jew half-way, the bridge will not be complete.

Increasingly the stress is on the Christian Approach of the local church to the Jew ;  but though lip service is paid to the principle, the objection is repeatedly raised that in practice it is difficult or even impossible for the local church to establish the necessary contacts without compromising its Christian position.  If encouraged, such Hebrew Christian bridge-building efforts which include a fair proportion of Gentile Christians could go far towards solving the problem, and would do much in addition to help the local church to understand its Hebrew Christians.

## A Deep Longing for Genuine Christian Unity

At all times there have been deep divisions and wide differences of opinion in Jewry.  Opinions to the contrary are due to the widespread ignorance of matters Jewish in Christendom as a whole.  But however deep the differences and however bitter the feelings they might arouse, it was only on the rarest occasions that they were not transcended by the realization of common membership in the people of God.

This sense of Jewish unity deep down in spite of all superficial difference has been strengthened, we need hardly add, by the centuries of persecution through which the Jew has passed. Another influence has been the relative unimportance of theology and theological controversy in Jewish thought compared with Christianity.

The frequent Jewish objection to the truth of Christianity on the basis of Christian disunity is not merely a propaganda pose. Nothing comes as a greater shock to the average convert than to discover how deep Christian divisions go and that denominational differences often count for more than a common faith in Christ. Then the day often comes when he finds these purely man-made barriers coming between him and some other convert from Judaism, and the position we so often take for granted becomes for him intolerable.

For so many Gentile Christians, brought up as they are in implicitly accepted denominational loyalties, ecumenical principles tend often to be no more than pious platitudes. But for the Hebrew Christian, for whom faith in Christ is more important than the theology in which it is expressed, and the worship of the heart more important than its outward forms, the unity of the Church is something vital. Nothing has hurt him more than the deep-rooted and far-reaching differences between Christians, not even the lack of understanding for him by so many, or the active dislike of the Jew by some.

Though it is fashionable in the Church to give lip-service to the cause of Christian unity, there are comparatively few who really welcome the man who takes it seriously. For all that, the unity of the Church is a spiritual necessity, however the Spirit of God may lead us to it. In the mission field the demands of the indigenous churches are increasingly bringing this unity into existence. It may be that, as the churches at home come to understand the vision of unity the Lord of the Church has given the Hebrew Christian, he will prove one of the means for making unity a reality in our midst.

A Genuine and often Well-Founded Dislike of much
that is Usual in Gentile Churches

The deepest revolt of many Hebrew Christians against
the system in which they find themselves is, however,
against its theology and practice, and this will be found
especially among those for whom nationality means least.

Today in theological circles it is becoming a commonplace
that, however much the Church may have gained from
Greek thought, this has been a corruption of the Hebraic
form in which it pleased God to reveal Himself. But it is
one thing to recognize this theoretically, altogether another
to root out of our thinking and of the thinking of our
churches the traditions of centuries. Greek thought has
coloured our theological thinking through and through,
and we need someone reared in another tradition to show
us how far the injection of this Hellenic germ has penetrated
the system.

The indigenous churches of the mission field often
provide this challenge, but it tends to be negative and
destructive, for the Hebrew form of thought comes no more
naturally to them than it does to us. Lev Gillet [1] was quite
correct in stressing what the Church could learn from the
Synagogue and from Jewish tradition, and in maintaining
that a revival of Hebrew Christianity could mean the
restoration of many lost riches to the Church. It may well
be that, as the Holy Spirit gradually leads the Hebrew
Christians in the land of Israel to a greater unity and to
a deeper understanding of their faith, an indigenous Hebrew
Christian Church will arise that will have a fertilizing
influence on the Church as a whole. But until that day
comes we have the Hebrew Christian in our midst from
whom we may learn.

All too often in the past the questions and difficulties of
the Hebrew Christian have been looked on as evidence for
a double dose of original sin and a questionable conversion.
It would be very foolish to go to the other extreme and to
assume that he is always correct in his questions and

[1] *Communion in the Messiah.*

difficulties.  But if the local church is willing to pay the price of having some of its most cherished convictions challenged, it may find in the Hebrew Christian the means of freeing it from much dead tradition, and for leading it to a much deeper and richer understanding of God.

The challenge of the Hebrew Christian to the practice of the Church goes further and is more important than his challenge to its theology.  James Parkes writes very well, ' Somehow the balance has to be retained which recognizes the supreme tragedy involved for Judaism in the rejection of Jesus ; but this can only result from the parallel recognition of the second tragedy which followed later, when the followers of Jesus rejected the real essentials of Sinai, a rejection which has left the Church impotent in the face of the breakdown of the modern world '.[1]  All too often the Sermon on the Mount is the least honoured portion of the Gospel, the stern ethics of the Old Testament prophets are replaced by sentimentality, and the community of the synagogue by the organization of the church.

Modern man, so often the victim of economic circumstances, with the old fixed landmarks of right and wrong obliterated, and feeling desperately lonely with the fragmentation of the community and even of the family in our modern urban civilization, turns to the Church in his need. He may well receive the right answer, but so often he cannot see any effort made to put that answer into practice ; no attempt is made to carry the teaching of Sinai into effect.  And so Communism challenges the Church and all too often seems to win, not because of the strength of its case, but because the Church has failed to carry its own teaching into effect.

Here again the Hebrew Christian may well serve as the awakener of the Church's conscience and the bearer of a renewed vision of social righteousness.

In brief, if the Church will look on the Hebrew Christian with his foibles and difficulties neither as a curiosity nor as a nuisance, nor yet as a danger and a potential heresiarch,

---

[1] *Judaism and Christianity*, p. 42.

but as a problem to be solved for the glory of God, the Church itself will derive blessing from its patience and understanding. The Hebrew Christian is perfect neither in life nor in thought, and his motives sometimes leave something to be desired, but he is a brother in Christ, and his main difficulties are primarily of the Church's own creation. The Israel out of which he has come has largely been moulded by its century-long persecution at the hands of official Christendom, while the new Israel into which he has come may all too often show few of the marks of the Body of Christ. Even as the continued existence of the Jew in his refusal of Christ constitutes the supreme challenge to the missionary vocation of the Church, so the Hebrew Christian in its midst is its supreme challenge that it should recapture the mind of its Lord for its organization, living, theology, and outlook. The better he can preserve his existence and individuality, the greater will be his contribution to the universal Church.

# IX

THE SPECIFIC RESPONSIBILITY OF THE CHURCH AND THE
LOCAL CONGREGATION TO THE JEWS TODAY

## 1. HOW FAR HAS THE CHURCH ACCEPTED ITS RESPONSIBILITY?

GÖTE HEDENQUIST

THE Amsterdam Conference of the World Council of Churches in 1948 brought to many churches an incitement to quite a changed attitude in their contact both with the Jewish people and with individual Jews living within the local areas of the churches. In some parts of the world the ' parish approach ' to the Jews has been stressed long before. But now a more or less common policy and strategy could be agreed upon so far as the attitude of the Churches to the Jews was concerned. This does not mean that all Churches now feel the same responsibility for their Jewish neighbours. But in some cases the recommendations from Amsterdam really meant an awakening in Churches and parishes to this new responsibility.

On the one hand, there had formerly been a gap between the Christian parishes and the Jewish communities, in some countries due to antisemitic ideas and feelings among the people of the country concerned and the influence of such ideas on many Church members. On the other hand, to many Church members there had seemed to be no great difference between the Christian and Jewish believers. They had the same God, most of the Bible in common, and the same Holy Land was theirs. Christ and Messiah received just a secondary place in the thinking of such Christians.

The Amsterdam recommendations to the member

Churches of the World Council of Churches, however, made it quite clear that the first and main task and responsibility of the Churches towards the Jews was an evangelistic and missionary one. Co-operation and friendship between Christians and Jews should be self-evident, but never should this create any barriers to witnessing for the Gospel among the Jews.

As in the latter-day missionary work among the Gentiles, the Christian Approach to the Jews was started by voluntary missionary societies, more or less connected with their home Churches. The work in the home field by those societies, designed to arouse interest among the Church people in this missionary task, has led many Churches nowadays to regard these missionary societies as being the appropriate official or unofficial channel for missionary work among the Jews. This is, for instance, the case in the Scandinavian countries, in England, and in Germany. In other countries the Church has felt its own responsibility for this work and given the Christian Approach to the Jews a central part in its own organization. This is the case in some Churches in U.S.A., in Scotland, in Holland, and during recent years in Austria.

A quite unique position so far as the Christian Approach to the Jews is concerned is taken by the *State of Israel*. Here for the first time we have a country where the Jewish population is in the majority and the Christians form a very small non-conformed minority. More than in other countries, the Christian Approach to the Jews here will have to arise from conversation between individual Christians and Jews on a theological, moral, or practical level. Individual Protestant Christians scattered over the land of Israel seem to direct their thinking and desires towards the founding of a Christian Church in Israel as time goes on.

If we look at developments in some European countries and Churches, we will find that in *Europe* generally the attitude of the Church towards the Jews during the last years has changed considerably, due to the fact that before and during World War II most of the European Jews were annihilated by the Nazis or emigrated to other continents.

Out of seven million Jews in Europe (outside U.S.S.R.) before the War, there are now about one million. In the countries west of the ' iron curtain ' there are about 900,000, half of which number are in England and 240,000 in France. That means that in the former Nazi-influenced countries, such as Germany and Austria, the number is a very small one, not considered ' dangerous ' to the populations of those countries. The Churches in those countries, no longer oppressed by any antisemitic régime, have on several occasions shown real interest in a positive Christian attitude from the Church people towards the Jews.

In *Germany* the evangelical Church at a synod in Berlin, 23rd to 27th April, 1950, published a resolution indicating to Church members what leading Churchmen thought of the cruelties against the Jews during the Nazi period and the necessity of a change in thinking and behaviour on the part of Christians towards their Jewish neighbours. This resolution says :

> We believe in the Lord and Saviour, who as man came from the Jewish people. We belong to the Church that is composed of Jewish Christians and Gentile Christians in one body and whose peace is Jesus Christ. We believe that promises by God to His chosen people Israel are equally valid even after the crucifixion of Jesus Christ. We confess openly that we by failure and silence are guilty before the God of mercy, of the crime that has been committed against the Jews by men of our people. We pray all Christians to make themselves free from antisemitism whatever source it may have, and earnestly defeat it where it rises anew, and to meet Jews, and Christians of Jewish origin, in the true fellowship of the spirit of Christ.

This declaration from the leading evangelical churches in Germany has meant very much to the Church people both inside Germany and outside. Another sign of a changed attitude towards the Jews among the German people can be seen in the activities of ' Peace with Israel ', which is planning to collect in Germany the means for planting six million olive trees in the land of Israel, each one being a monument to a Jew killed by the German National Socialists.

Direct missionary work among the Jews in Germany is also carried out by a number of missionary societies and organizations, joined in the Evangelical Committee for Service to Israel.

In *Austria* the Evangelical Church, according to the Amsterdam recommendations, has taken up evangelism among the Jews as part of the Church work. An Austrian pastor has been appointed to be responsible for this work in the Lutheran Church in Austria, in close co-operation with the Swedish Mission to the Jews in Vienna, which has been doing such work in Austria since about 1920. A declaration from a synod of the superintendents in the Austrian Lutheran Church in May 1952 was sent to all Lutheran pastors and Church workers in that country, in order to awaken and stimulate their interest in evangelism among the Jews.

Even in *Hungary*, the parish approach to the Jews is going on in the organization ' The Good Shepherd ', to judge by the somewhat meagre reports. In *Rumania, Czechoslovakia,* and *Poland* all organized missionary work among the Jews seems to have ceased, owing to the present political situation.

No organized missionary work among the Jews has been reported from the Protestant Churches in *Italy,* nor in *Spain* or *Portugal.* In Italy foreign missionary societies have been invited to start work among the Jews, but so far nothing has been achieved.

In *Switzerland* a special missionary society is trying to rouse interest in evangelism among the Jews on the home field, and is also trying to cover a part of the former field of the Basel Mission in the south of Germany.

The Protestant Churches in *France* have set up a common Committee for the Christian Approach to the Jews, but that Committee seems to be more a source of information than of really active evangelism among the Jews on the part of the Churches. From one Church in that country the answer was received that the members of the Church did not favour the missionary approach to the Jews, or evangelism among the Jews, for fear of offending the Jewish communities with whom contact and co-operation

had been established.  In Paris to a large extent the missionary work among the Jews has been carried out by the
Swedish Mission to the Jews.

In *Holland* during the last few years the Hervormde Kerk
in its Church Law has included the Christian Approach to
the Jews as a part of regular Church activity.  Direct
missionary work or evangelism is not stressed, but conversation with the Jews is emphasized as a means of witnessing
to the Gospel.  Very well organized missionary work
among the Jews both in Holland and in Belgium is also
carried on by the Gereformeerde Kerk in Holland.

Half of the Jews in Western Europe today are living in
*England*, about 450,000.  A number of missionary societies,
acting jointly in the Committee on Work among the Jews of
the Conference of Missionary Societies in Great Britain
and Ireland, are the channels for a great interest on the
part of many ministers and Church members.  The Church
of England has published, through its Church Missions
to Jews, a pamphlet called *The Jew in the Parish*, in which
the recommendations from the Amsterdam Assembly are
commended to ministers and Church members.  Most of
the Churches have their own missionary societies for work
among the Jews, stressing both the parish approach and
the foreign missionary work among the Jews.  The Church
of *Scotland* has formed a special Committee for the Christian
Approach to the Jews ;  it consists of one representative
from each parish, and is an integral part of the Church of
Scotland.

In the *Scandinavian countries* the interest in the Jewish
people has been a part of the revival movement of the last
century in the Churches, and is carried forward by missionary societies deeply anchored in the Church life.  The
main task of these missionary societies has been foreign
missionary work among the Jews, since the Jewish population in the Scandinavian countries is a rather small one.
The forces have been concentrated in some European
countries, in North Africa, and in the land of Israel.  On
the home field these societies have been of great help to
the Churches in giving information about Jewish questions,

in stimulating biblical and theological interest in the Jews, and in emphasizing that the Jews are a responsibility of the Churches.

Many European missionary societies have the twofold task of approaching the Churches in their homelands to arouse and maintain a real interest in the Christian Approach to the Jews, and secondly of approaching the Jews in countries where there are no Churches or where the indigenous Churches cannot do the evangelistic or missionary work among the Jews. The Church of England through the Church Missions to Jews is carrying out missionary work in Morocco, Algiers, Tunis, and Egypt as well as in Israel and Persia. The British Jews Society (of partly Baptist background) is doing missionary work in South Africa, South America, Australia, and Israel. The Church of Scotland is maintaining churches, a hospital, and a school in Israel. All Scandinavian missionary societies concerned with the Jews have work in Israel, the Danes and Swedes in North Africa also, and the Swedes in Austria and France. This foreign missionary activity is due to the fact that, in spite of the number of Jews being rather high in those areas, either no indigenous Church has been able to take up organized work among those Jews or help is badly needed.

In *Israel* there are now about one and a half million Jews and in the rest of *Asia* about half a million. In *Africa* the number is considered to be about 600,000, mainly in the northern and southern parts of the Continent.

In *South America* there are about 700,000 Jews and in *Australia* about 50,000.

The main interest nowadays, at least spiritually, is concentrated on the land of Israel but it must not be forgotten that about half of world Jewry today is living in the *United States of America*, where there are about five million Jews. This is in fact less than 3 per cent of the whole population in U.S.A. ; but if we take into consideration the fact that, of these five million, about two million are living in New York City and most of the others in cities with a population of more than 100,000, we understand the great influence of this Jewish world on American public opinion. That does not mean that American Jewry is a unit. In fact less than 50 per cent have any connection with a religious community or a Synagogue. Most of them have lost contact with their Jewish institutions during years of escape and refugee life, and become just secularized modern people with the one main interest of earning their living and enjoying life. Here the responsibility of the churches has grown tremendously, parallel to the growing opportunities for a real Christian Approach to the Jews.

Some of the Churches in U.S.A. have seen the responsibility and opportunity. The National Lutheran Council has established a special 'Department for the Christian Approach to the Jewish People'. From the central office in Chicago this department has organized missionary work all over the country through wholetime appointed ministers, who are trying to help the parish ministers with advice and counsel in their parish approach to the Jews. The main emphasis is on creating among the parish ministers and the parish members a positive interest in evangelism among the Jews. Every individual Christian will have to be a missionary. Of the 9500 Lutheran parishes in U.S.A., about 4000 have some Jewish population within the area of activity of the parish minister. Of these parishes 37·7 per cent have stated that there is a positive relationship between Church members and their Jewish neighbours, and there is some kind of evangelism or missionary work going on among the Jews. Through the central office, literature has been produced for ministers and parish members, and also pamphlets to be put into the hands of the Jews. The reports show that a clear theological basis is necessary for sound missionary work among the Jews. But the efforts already made also have shown that the Jews themselves look more respectfully upon missionary work or evangelism done by a Christian Church than on a single missionary on his own behalf trying to gather a group around himself. An enquiry addressed to a number of American rabbis has shown that the rabbis generally understand the missionary work as being an expression of the very nature of the Church. 'Since Christianity is a missionary religion', writes one rabbi, ' you have not only a right but a duty to include the Jews in your evangelistic programme.'   Another rabbi says :   ' After all, if you sincerely believe that you possess the means of human salvation, it seems to me that you must consider it your duty to make that truth available to the largest number of people '.   It was only to some of the methods of missionary work among the Jews that these rabbis declared themselves to be opposed.

A very great interest in evangelism or missionary work among the Jews is also shown by the Presbyterian Church in U.S.A., which has organized an approach to the Jews as a part of the Church work in industrial centres, and among other things has published a number of pamphlets both for Church members and for Jews.   Other American Churches having ministers specially appointed for evangelism among the Jews are the Reformed Church and the Congregational Church.

In *Canada* the Anglican Church is sponsoring a minister and a deaconess, appointed for rousing interest among the students of Universities, and the Women's Inter-Church Council is giving a large part of its programme to the Christian Approach to the Jews.

To most American Christians, however, it does not make any sense to talk about evangelism among the Jews.   To them a friendly attitude towards the Jews is the principal Christian duty.   ' Why should we evangelize among the Jews, who believe in the same God as we do ?   We have to bring the Gospel to those who do not know God.'   This is the usual answer.   And even if there is a feeling of responsibility for evangelism among the Jews, there is still the question for many as to where this evangelism will have to begin.   ' Should we try to convert Jews who have their religious home in the Synagogue ?   Or should we approach the secularized Jews ? '   One answer to these questions has been given by *the American Committee on the Christian Approach to the Jews*, representing all Protestant Churches in U.S.A., in its ' Aims and Basis ', paragraph IV of which reads :

We aim to promote, by all possible and ethically fair means, goodwill, understanding, and co-operation between Christians and Jews. While we fully appreciate the value and necessity of such goodwill and neighbour-liness, and endorse and urge active promotion of such, we would emphasize the fact that the full Christian obligation toward the Jewish people involves, in addition, the presentation of the claims of Christ to them as to all peoples. Our commission is to teach, to preach, and to share Jesus Christ in boldness of faith to all men.

Although this statement is quite clear, there is still much uncertainty among American Church people as to the Christian Approach to the Jews. On the one hand, there seems to them to be no danger in bridging all the differences between the Jewish and the Christian faiths, thus achieving some kind of a syncretism. On the other hand, both Christians and Jews seem to want the distinction between their two religions to stay permanently. But many Christian parish members do not seem to regard their own religion as the absolute religion. Nor do they think of God as essentially the Father of Jesus Christ, to whom nobody comes but by Him !

In other groups of Christians in America it has become quite evident that a growing interest in the Christian Approach to the Jews has also caused a deeper under-standing of the Bible as a whole. This is probably true not only of American Christians but also of Christians all over the world.

Here ministers and other Church workers in all Churches have their great responsibility. It might be true, as an American pastor has said, that we need a revival in our Churches first ; and then evangelism among the Jews will follow naturally. But it is equally true that the interest in the Christian Approach to the Jews can give a new and deepened understanding of the Bible and thus cause a revival in the life of Church members. I have seen some-thing of this myself during the Nazi persecution of the Jews in Germany and Austria before and during World War II. For that reason it is an important task for all ministers to create such an interest among their parish members in the Christian Approach to the Jews.

RESPONSIBILITY OF CHURCH TO JEWS    177

In some Churches, in both Europe and U.S.A., the main
task in the creation of this initial interest was considered to
be the publication of literature giving some facts about the
Biblical and theological background of this kind of evangel-
ism, and teaching people how to approach a Jew in a
Christian way.   One of the most excellent booklets of that
kind, entitled *What about Anti-Semitism?* was produced by
the Women's Missionary Society of the United Lutheran
Church in America in 1950, and is available from the
Department for the Christian Approach to the Jewish
People, National Lutheran Council, 327 S. LaSalle Street,
Chicago 4, Illinois.   It contains in 78 pages ' Seven Forum
Programs ' on the Christian Approach to the Jews, giving
facts about the Jews in U.S.A. and stressing the responsibility of the Churches towards the Jews ;  it is based upon
the Biblical teaching and tries to show means of contact
between parish members and Jews in order not to hide
Christ from the Jews, but to reveal Him to them.   The
same Department for the Christian Approach to the Jewish
People of the National Lutheran Council in U.S.A. has
published a number of similar booklets available without
charge from the same address.   It would, however, be of
great value if many more Churches in America would
make more use of such publications in order to increase
knowledge of and arouse more interest in the Christian
Approach to the Jews.

The same applies to the situation all over the world.
At the last two annual meetings of the *International Missionary
Council's Committee on the Christian Approach to the Jews* the
need for literature was emphasized, and both Missionary
Societies and Churches have been urged to promote high-
standard books and pamphlets on this subject, to be put
into the hands of both ministers and other Church members.
Special action has been undertaken by the same committee
to produce Christian literature in the Hebrew language
in the land of Israel.

There is also another way in which Churches and
Missionary Societies have shown their interest in and
understanding of the importance of the Christian Approach

12

to the Jews. The more the responsibility for this kind of evangelism has been acknowledged, the more the lack of knowledge and the need of instruction for ministers and other church workers has been felt. For that reason the *Summer Courses on the Church and the Jews* arranged every second year by the International Missionary Council's Committee on the Christian Approach to the Jews have attracted an increasing number of students. The last one, in Germany in 1952, was attended by 70 students from 15 countries. It is also the hope of the Committee that the *two permanent Christian institutes for Jewish studies*—Institutum Judaicum Delitschianum in Münster, Germany, and the Swedish Theological Institute in Jerusalem, Israel—will become more widely known, in order to be of more help to the Churches in providing ministers and students with information and guidance on the relationship between the Church and the Jews. Applications for scholarships at the Institute in Jerusalem can be sent in to the Director of the International Missionary Council's Committee on the Christian Approach to the Jews, New York or London.

The Christian Approach to the Jews is still in some Churches and countries looked upon as an interest maintained by a few narrow-minded Christians who see in the creation of the new State of Israel a kind of fulfilment of God's promises to His chosen people. It is, however, the hope of the writer of this chapter that more leading churchmen will become aware of the fact that the Christian Approach to the Jews must be a common concern of all Churches. This kind of evangelism touches a central nerve in the teaching and preaching of the Churches, and has been thus acknowledged by some Churches. No Church or denomination should fail to accept the Christian Approach to the Jews as a natural part of its Church programme, and an expression of its Church activity in Christian evangelism.

## 2. THE APPROACH OF THE LOCAL CHURCH

### W. A. CURTIS

No Christian would deny that the Christian religion is for all mankind, for everyone of whatever race or colour, but it is something of which we need to be continually reminded. This is particularly so as regards the Jews, for there are approximately half a million Jews in Britain, generally concentrated in our cities and large towns but also to be found in lesser numbers in many smaller towns and villages. We may not think it as urgent to present the Gospel to them as to others in our parishes, we may fight shy of having anything to do with trying to convert the Jew because of the difficulty of the task or dislike of him ; but whatever the reason for neglecting this duty, we are bound to admit it is something we ought to do.

During the outburst of missionary enthusiasm at the beginning of the last century some people felt called to this particular task of converting the Jews, and their first thought was for the Jew in their midst. In fact the Jewish Missionary Societies in this country started as an attempt to evangelize the Jews in London. This work was done by people who were specially trained, made special efforts, had special meetings, special study groups and services, and by these methods large numbers of Jews were contacted and many found their way to a knowledge of Jesus Christ as their Saviour. Since then a small but steady stream of men and women have responded to this call and the impressive list of outstanding Hebrew Christians of the past hundred and fifty years bears testimony to the effectiveness of this work. These efforts were made by the parish or by outside workers, either as an addition to or independent of the parish activities. A number of interdenominational missions to the Jews were also established, and these have centres in most of our cities and large towns.

One parish where a special effort was made for the Jewish parishioners was All Saints', Buxton Street, in the East End of London, where the Jews comprised nearly half the population of the parish. The Vicar, the Rev. Basil Rust, in his book published in 1901 describes how workers, specially assigned to this task and specially trained, took the good news of the Gospel to the Jews by means of clinics and schools.

Doubts have arisen in recent years, however, as to whether this is the most effective method for the average parish today. There are a few parishes where the Jews are in such large numbers that the special effort by specially trained workers may still be the best method of approach, and some parishes use this method today ; but since the War, although the numbers of Jews in this country have increased, they have become more widespread throughout the country, with the result that a much more common question for a parish is how to approach the comparatively few Jews it numbers among its parishioners. A special effort in every place where there are Jews would obviously be impossible, but here in Britain we are fortunate in having ready to hand in our parochial system an effective means of approaching the Jew. To make use of the parish, its Church services and organizations as a means of approaching the Jews has not been given much consideration until fairly recently, but an increasing number are trying to do something in this way about their Jewish parishioners, though the number is only a small fraction of the whole.

FIRST CONSIDERATIONS

In considering the general question of approaching Jews in such parishes where they are not a substantial part of the population there are at the outset two main points to be made.

The first is that the Jews are a special case. There are many reasons why they must be considered such, the strongest and most obvious being dislike of the Jew. This is generally not bitter nor deep-seated, but it is widespread and often found within our churches. Much has been written about this complicated question ; but whatever the rights and wrongs of it are, its existence is a fact with which we have to contend. All prejudice is un-Christian, but prejudice against the Jew has existed for so long that it needs a special effort on the part of the Christian to resolve it. But resolved it must be before a Christian can commend the Gospel to a Jew.

Among other reasons for the Jews being a special case is the fact that they already have a religion and a good one ; in fact until two thousand years ago it was the best religion in the world, a religion revealed to them by God in preparation for the coming of God Himself into the world. They also have a very strong sense of loyalty to family, community, race, and religion, which presents a formidable obstacle to their acknowledging the claims of the Christian Gospel, and this often means paying a price, which includes the loss of affection and respect of family and friends, for professing the Christian faith. They are a people, too, whose history cannot be completely explained in the usual terms of historical development ; and though varying in the extent of their assimilation, they are in origin and outlook a different people from us.

But the second and equally important point is that though the Jew is a special case it must not appear that he is being treated as such, for if he thought he was being made a special object of evangelism it would cause a great deal of unnecessary opposition. For this reason any parochial approach to the Jew must be done without advertisement, for it has been proved over and over again that publication of details of work done in any particular parish has an adverse effect upon that work.

This article, based on reports of what has been done in some parishes in Britain, must therefore suffer from a withholding of details, which would make the account more interesting but might ill affect the work which is being done at present.

## Its Difficulties

Parishes which have tried the parochial approach agree that any effort must begin by making it clear that prejudice against the Jew is un-Christian and must give way to informed opinion and a willingness to try and understand. Like all prejudice, this one is due largely to ignorance and misrepresentation, and only after it is dispelled can any effective effort be made to approach the Jew in the right Christian spirit, and thus try in turn to dispel the prejudice the Jew has about the Christian faith.

Mention must be made here of the work of the Council of Christians and Jews, which was formed for this one purpose of dispelling prejudice and succeeds in doing a tremendous amount of good in this respect by bringing Christians and Jews together in an atmosphere of friendliness and fellowship. Christians must applaud the effort at better understanding between Jews and Christians provided it is made clear that the object of the Council is a limited one and should not be thought of as a substitute for evangelism. A branch of the Council of Christians and Jews in a parish does not meet the Christian obligation of the parish to proclaim the Gospel to the Jews, for the Council of Christians and Jews brings Christians and Jews together in order that prejudice may be dispelled, while the Parochial Approach aims at dispelling prejudice in order that the message of the Gospel may be proclaimed more clearly.

With the exception of the Moslems, the Jews are considered to be the most difficult people to evangelize, and they therefore constitute the supreme challenge to the Christians in a parish. The Synagogue stands as a challenge to the Church and is a sign of the ineffectiveness of our witness to the Jews. The Jew being a supreme test of our efforts to spread the Gospel, there is a strong temptation to leave him for other and easier objectives. With so much to do in a parish, with overworked clergy and church workers fully occupied with the many various parochial activities, this is a real temptation. The Parochial Approach therefore is limited to those parishes where the clergy are prepared to take on this extra work and try to get the necessary co-operation from members of the congregation.

## And Its Compensations

But the task of approaching the Jews has its compensations too. One advantage of tackling the Jews through the Parochial Approach is that learning something of the Jews and their religion, in preparation for such a task, makes for a better understanding of the Christian faith. One's own faith becomes more clear when defending it against a worthy adversary. In addition, to gain Jews for Christ will enrich the Church with people who, in religion, are endowed above the average and who can help others to a better understanding of the religion in which Our Lord Himself was brought up. Much of the New Testament, including many of Our Lord's own words, can be made more clear by a Jew with his intimate knowledge of the faith and practices of Judaism.

## What is Being Done

The answer to the question as to what extent the Parochial Approach is being tried in this country is a disappointing one, though requests for advice and suitable literature show that advantage is being taken of some of the contacts made with Jews. Though there are no records the numbers of Jews found in our Churches indicate that in some parishes they are included in the normal parish ministrations.

There are a few parishes where a missionary society has provided a worker with a special knowledge of the Jews and of the best way to approach them. These workers have been taken on as ordinary members of the staff and take their full part in the work of the parish, but are able to give particular attention to those Jews with whom contact has been made.

In two of our cities two specially trained workers give all their time to Jewish work, trying to contact Jews by whatever means are available and then putting the enquirers into touch with their particular parish church.

Other parishes have made their own special efforts without any outside help, and the following is an account of what is happening in some parishes, most of them in London.

During the War Jewish refugees from the Continent, who were attempting to settle down in London, were invited to a Church Hall for a series of musical evenings. The average attendance was about a hundred. No attempt was made to preach the Gospel at all by word, although it was made clear that the invitation was in the name of the Church, and because the Christian community felt that it would like to do something to help the newcomers to the district. In addition to this, in the post-War years when antisemitism made itself felt, the church, in the name of Jesus Christ, denounced it at open meetings convened for that purpose. The sympathy aroused for the church among the Jews was overwhelming, and in consequence at that particular church there has never ceased to be a trickle of men and women who were lost to Judaism, finding their way to the inner Church fellowship through baptism and confirmation.

At another church between fifty and sixty Jews and Christians in about equal proportions meet once a month in a Church Hall, for a lecture on some aspect of Judaism, or Christianity, or a Brains Trust, or some other social activity. In general the more serious items are preferred. The result of this attempt by the church to bring Jews and Christians together in friendly contact has meant a new respect for the Church in that parish and district, and a willingness to listen to its message ; and, as in the first example given above, individual Jews are beginning to find their way to the vicar for guidance in the Christian faith.

A valuable point of contact has been made in one parish by attempting to sell parish magazines to Jewish households as well as Gentile. Parish magazines are often readily accepted by Jews, and the fact that they are read in not a few cases has been proved by donations sent to the church by Jews in response to appeals made. Valuable work could be done in many parishes where there is a Jewish population, if articles from a Christian viewpoint were written by someone with a knowledge of Jewish interests.

In one East London parish the vicar printed a series of letters to all his parishioners, giving an especially warm welcome to the Jewish neighbours, inviting them to a social in the Church Hall. The letters were delivered to the various houses by hand and the response from the Jews was most encouraging from the point of view of numbers and of the points of contact made.

As prejudice against the Jews is frequently the product of ignorance an attempt is made, in one East London parish, to strangle antisemitism at birth by taking Gentile schoolchildren to the local synagogue to explain Jewish forms of worship. Schoolchildren are not usually given to racial or other prejudices, and schools present a valuable opportunity for anticipating any prejudice the children may meet in later years. At one public school where the only Jewish scholar was diffident about any public observances of his religion, the chaplain felt that the best way of commending Christian tolerance was to arrange for the boy to be instructed by a rabbi once a week. It also helped the other scholars to see that faiths other than their own must be respected. In such an atmosphere the merits of different creeds can be discussed and thus the seeds of evangelism sown.

It is undoubtedly true that a valuable means of evangelism, particularly in a Jewish area, is the maintenance of a Church School. If it is wisely run, it is not unusual for the Jewish children to attend Christian worship and Christian instruction. The experience of schools varies a good deal in this matter, depending on the form of Judaism professed in the locality. In areas where the Jews are liberal it is not uncommon for nine out of every ten Jewish children who attend the school to join in the Christian worship and instruction, although the parents are given the option of withdrawing them. This is true for Primary

Schools. When children reach Secondary School age, however, there is a much greater degree of keenness on the part of Jewish parents to withdraw their children. The fact, however, remains that a number of Jews who have come to an experience of the Christian way of life in later years trace the beginning of this movement to their contact with a Christian school.

In two parishes the young people were asked to do something about the Jewish parishioners. After a series of talks to the Youth Fellowship on Jewish history, anti-semitism, and the religion of Judaism, a few of the members offered to make it their special task in the parish to bring Jews into the Fellowship and thus into the Church. There was no publicity and nothing was organized, except that these people met regularly for prayer.

During the Mission to London a number of people were conscious of the need to present the challenge to the Jews as well as to others who were outside the Church. To help those who had volunteered to visit in preparation for this evangelistic campaign, a number of letters were printed, including a special one to be given to Jews making it clear that they would be as welcome as anyone else at the services and meetings because ' the Christian faith transcends all national and racial barriers and its message of salvation is for EVERY man '. This was repeated as part of the more recent Mission to Hull.


LITERATURE

Among the books which have been found useful to give to Jewish enquirers there is *Why Men Believe in Jesus Christ*, by Rev. D. W. Cleverley Ford (price 3s. 6d.), an account of Our Lord's life written, though it does not say so, with the Jewish enquirer in mind ; and *The Jew and Jesus Christ*, by Dr J. Jocz (price 21s.), certain chapters of which are very pertinent for Jewish enquirers. As a general rule, however, it is found best to try and get the Jew to begin by reading the New Testament itself, and there is a very helpful version of St Matthew's Gospel by Einsbruch with all quotations from the Old Testament in Hebrew. There is also a Hebrew-English parallel New Testament.

In conclusion, reference should be made to a recent change in the general attitude of those who approach the Jews. Instead of denouncing the shortcomings of the Jewish faith and accusing the Jews of blindness of heart for not accepting Jesus as their Messiah, the tendency is rather to begin by agreeing that there is much misunderstanding on both sides, that the Jewish religion has a great deal of the truth concerning God, and that Christians should be grateful for all that the Jews have done to prepare for the coming of Jesus and in nurturing the Christian Church in its first years. In thus emphasizing at the beginning the good points of Judaism the way is better prepared for showing later that what the faith of Judaism lacks can be filled only by acceptance of Our Lord Jesus Christ as Saviour and Messiah.

## An Essential Element

While the Parochial Approach is an effort made within the framework of a parish and its organizations, its essential basis is the attempt by individual Christians to reach out to individual Jews, and there is no substitute for this. One must, therefore, take for granted that behind any account of the Parochial Approach there are these ordinary stories of contacts made and followed up, with, by God's grace, sometimes a subsequent bringing of someone into the fellowship of the parish and the Church, and we quote two examples representing the essential part of the Parochial Approach.

A young Jew came as a stranger to a London vicar and asked how long it would take to make him a Christian, as he wanted to marry a Gentile. This vicar pointed out very kindly that he could explain the Christian faith but it is God alone who can make anyone a Christian. The young man came to church and attended a small instruction class for nearly a year, but no real progress was made. Then the girl he was to marry changed her mind, and this crisis brought the young man to a decision. After a short break he resumed attendance at the classes but was coming now, he said, because he had found the Lord Jesus Christ. He finished his University course and started his career and is now in another part of the country, living with a Christian family, and making his witness as a full member in his new parish.

A young Jewess from a good home and of good education was reserved and shy and not happy at her work. A parish worker heard about her and was able to make her acquaintance. After over a year's friendship she was persuaded to go to a Bible Study group and later attended Confirmation classes. She is now a confirmed Christian and happy in her new-found faith.

God alone can call and convert ; the individual Christian can, by patient showing of Christian love and understanding, dispel the prejudice and fear that prevent the call of God from being clearly heard and the truth of the Gospel from being clearly seen.

X

# THE CHRISTIAN MESSAGE TO ISRAEL

Robert Smith

THE title of this chapter assumes that the Church has a special concern for the Jewish people, which is the justification of the Christian approach. In an article written for *A Christian Year Book* (S.C.M. Press) the author gave a short definition which will be a convenient starting-point :

> The fundamental basis of this concern is the belief that the Gospel must be extended to the Jews on the same terms as to other peoples, and that no Church which discriminates against the Jews by withholding the Gospel can fulfil its function in the purpose of God. At the same time, the Church must realize that the unique history of the Jews, the place of Israel in God's design, and the peculiar position of the Jewish people in the world today, make necessary a special kind of approach, and differentiate the Church's responsibility to the Jews from its mission to other non-Christian peoples.

There are two contentions here which must be distinguished. The first will be generally admitted, at least in theory. It is almost a platitude in ecumenical circles. The Christian Gospel is universal. It applies to all men without exception. Therefore the Gospel must include the Jews. From the Christian standpoint no objection seems possible. The Jews can and do maintain that they have no need of Christ. But more amazing than the persistence of the Jews in their own religion has been the failure of the Church to accept any real responsibility for their evangelization. The logic of the Christian position has not prevented the neglect of the Christian approach to the Jews during many centuries of Church history and

189

in many lands where the Jews have sojourned in their world-wide dispersion. This failure leads us to suspect the logic of universalism as a motive power. In theory the belief in a universal Gospel should be enough to promote world-wide evangelization, which would take the Christian approach to the Jews in its stride. In practice, however, the Jews have been treated as an insignificant minority group, and the world missionary movement has been too big and too vague to concern itself with the people among whom Jesus Christ condescended to dwell. This must be recognized as a fundamental weakness of the ecumenical movement.

In actual fact it is only where a special concern has been felt, and where there has been some recognition of the place of Israel in God's design, that anything has been done about the Jews. Christian universalism is based not on rational propositions, such as the humanitarian principle that ' all men are born free and equal ', but on the will of God as revealed in the Gospel. It is only by accepting the terms of this revelation that the power of the Gospel can be made available for the whole world. And in this Gospel the place of the Jews is not subordinate or peripheral, but central.

It is at least doubtful whether a rational universalism has ever been the motive behind the Christian approach. In the long run a rational universalism cannot provide a basis for the missionary movement, and there seems to me to be a danger in the present emphasis on this line of thought, for example, in the reports of the Willingen Conference of the International Missionary Council.[1] It is true that the New Testament does arrive at the conviction that the Gospel is for all men, but the road to this belief is not the rational universalizing of God's love for individual human beings. The starting-point is the special concern of God for Israel, and the special revelation to the Jewish people of Jesus Christ, the Messiah. After the resurrection the disciples became convinced that the power of Jesus Christ was at work beyond the bounds of Israel according

[1] See the statement on the Missionary Obligation of the Church, p. 2 ff.

to the flesh, and that His life and death had a redemptive purpose for the whole world. This new conviction transformed but did not supersede their belief in God's special purpose for Israel. Both convictions are held together in the doctrine of the Church as the New Israel. This is well illustrated in J. B. Phillips' paraphrase of I Peter ii: 9: ' But you are God's " chosen generation ", His " royal priesthood ", His " holy nation ", His " peculiar people "— all the old titles of God's people now belong to you '. In other words, the privileges of Israel are extended as the Gospel of Christ is extended, but they are still privileges which belong to the Israel of God and can only be extended by His grace.

If there is any permanent truth in this view, then the distinction which the Jews themselves so stoutly maintain between Israel and the Gentile nations must be recognized as having some validity even for Christians. The Church cannot discriminate against the Jews by withholding the Gospel from them, but neither can it address them simply as human beings with no true religion. We must at least preface the message of the Gospel with a special message recognizing the distinction. In practice, of course, we adapt our message to our hearers according to their background. The Christian message to India or to Africa will differ in certain respects from preaching in the Older Churches. To the Jews we become as Jews, that we may gain the Jews. But in their case it is not merely a matte of expediency, a tactical change of approach to meet difficulties due to their peculiar circumstances and unfortunate history. If that were all, a strong case might be made out for ignoring the differences and treating the Jews like their neighbours, especially as many of them in the modern world are losing their traditions and are to all outward seeming just modern pagans. But if their history is in some sense part of the history of salvation, Christians must recognize it even when they themselves tend to forget it.

There is therefore a deeper theological motive for the Christian approach to the Jews : the recognition of God's purpose for Israel. The absence of this recognition largely accounts for the failure of the Church as a whole to undertake this task. The occasional interest in the Jews, which often took eccentric forms, has always gone hand in hand with an interest in the Old Testament revelation, in the doctrine of Israel's election, or in the uniqueness of the history of Israel. And it is a revival of these interests today that gives us promise of a more responsible attitude on the part of the Church. Without the light of this revelation the Church would continue to be blind to the existence of the Jews, and would stubbornly ignore or deny their uniqueness. Anti-semitism is the result of this blindness, for it is a form of resentment against the privileges of Israel, which are irrational not only to the nationalist but also to the universalist, and which can only assume meaning in the light of the knowledge of the will of God. The Christian approach to the Jews must start with a humble recognition of their place in God's plan, a reverent acceptance of the election of Israel.

The Church is still far from general agreement on these questions. The truth is often proclaimed only in a distorted form by sectarian witnesses. But there is a growing awareness of the following central truths:

(a) That the revelation on Mount Sinai and the Old Testament Covenant have real significance and continuing validity. There has been a profound change in the whole attitude to the Old Testament in recent years. It is no longer regarded as merely a source of primitive mythology and folk-lore. It is the prophetic revelation of God's eternal purpose. Thus Professor William Manson writes in an article in the *International Review of Missions* (July 1953):

> In reality [the New Covenant] represents the Old Covenant in its eschatological, at-last-complete accomplishment. The Exodus goes on. It is an eternal Divine event which announces itself afresh at all times of Divine illumination and crisis, and which will have its final realization in a New Age to come. The redemptive event of the Exodus underlies the Gospel of Jesus and the inauguration of the new era of Christianity.

I quote this as typical of the tone of much recent writing on the theology of the Old Testament.

(b) That Israel has a special mission in the Divine plan of salvation. At present theologians are more open to accept ' the scandal of particularity ' than were the idealists of an earlier generation. Many would now agree with Will Herberg, an American Jewish philosopher much influenced by Reinhold Niebuhr, when he writes in *Judaism and Modern Man* of the idealist rejection of the biblical doctrine of election :

> This is the stand of self-sufficient human reason, impatient of history and personality. Biblical faith, on the other hand, permeated with the inexpugnable particularity of existence, takes its stand on the affirmation : ' Salvation is of the Jews '.

It is notable that the major figures in the theology of all denominations, from Karl Barth and Reinhold Niebuhr to Berdyaev and Jacques Maritain, share this view.

(c) That Jewish and Christian history are interdependent. Since both Judaism and Christianity are historical revelations, the question of what constitutes the history of salvation is a serious one for both. Will Herberg states the question thus : ' There is no Judaism without Abraham and Moses, without Egypt and Sinai ; there is no Christianity without these and without Jesus and Calvary in addition '. It is obvious that this raises the further question for Christians: If Jesus and Calvary are the continuation of the Old Testament history, what about the post-Christian history of the Jews ? Is it also part of the history of salvation ? While for the Jews the question arises : If the revelation comes to us from Abraham and Moses, does it have nothing to do with Jesus and Calvary ? Why does our tradition by-pass the Christian continuation ?

(d) That antisemitism is a sin against Christ. At Amsterdam, antisemitism was denounced as ' absolutely irreconcilable with the profession or practice of the Christian faith ', and, such is the horror aroused by the mass crimes of Nazi racialism, no one is likely to dissent. There is need, however,

13

for a deeper recognition of Christian responsibility even for these crimes.

(e) That the Jews are a 'mystery' which can only be explained in the light of the Cross and of Christian eschatology. While this view is not so generally held, it is gaining ground, especially on the Continent : see, for example, Karl Hartenstein, *Israel im Heilsplan Gottes*. It does not seem so acceptable to the Anglo-Saxon mind, and it has its dangers. For it might be made an excuse for refusal to take responsibility for the Jews and their sufferings. On the other hand, this view recognizes the theological depth of the Jewish question, which cannot be explained in merely secular terms.

(f) The relationship between the Church and Israel should take the form of a dialogue. The new understanding of the meaning of Israel makes possible a much less one-sided contact between the Old Israel and the New. Until the Church becomes conscious of a common destiny with the Jews no real contact is in fact possible, and for this reason much of the missionary literature is now seen to be shadow-fighting. The Church must learn the meaning of its mission from the Old Israel, in order that it may teach the Jews the fulfilled meaning of their own history. ' In the Bible the conception of the Church's universal mission is bound up, first and last, with the thought of the Church being " the Israel of God " ' (W. Manson). On the other hand, it is not by detached and disinterested study or by a superficial exchange of compliments that this understanding grows, but only by the earnest desire that Israel may be saved, and by witnessing in this hour to the truth revealed in the history of salvation.

Thus the Church is called to re-examine its own mission and witness as the New Israel, to compare it with the original. If the claim is true, what are we doing to prove that we are the People of the Covenant ? In some respects the Jews seem to fulfil involuntarily the mission which the Church tries to carry out voluntarily. They are manifestly the Suffering Servant, the Cross-Bearers, although they cannot help themselves and have no choice. Similarly they appear often unconsciously and under pressure as a stimulating agency in earthly history, as if they existed to be ' the salt of the earth ', ' the light of the world '. The deliberate efforts of the Church to follow the commands of Christ in these respects often seem to be poor imitations. It is only when these facts have been fully recognized that the Church can approach the Jews as ambassadors of Christ.

(g) That the Church must explain the Jews to the world. It is only from the Christian standpoint that the Jews can be understood. The world has no category in which they belong. They are not a nation like other nations. Yet neither are they a people distinguished only by their religious beliefs. They are a people with a divine destiny, which they themselves cannot fully understand, because it is not yet manifest. Instinctively they look to Christians for protection ; for they live in the shelter of the Church, under the shadow of the Cross. Where the faith of the Bible flourishes, the Jews can find friends and interpreters. When the Church abandons the Jews to the world, the Church itself is in danger of being lost in the world.

Having dealt so far mainly with points of contact, let us now look at some of the main points of difference between the Church and Israel :

1. The traditional Christian message to Israel contrasts the Law and the Gospel. In the light of the biblical revelation this cannot be an absolute contrast. For the Law contains the promise of the Gospel, and the Gospel is the fulfilment of the Law. The Christian Church is not beyond all law, and often seems to be too much in bondage to its own laws. Nevertheless, it is plain that the Jews are in perplexity about the Law at the present time, and that the Christian message must give guidance on this issue. The former Prime Minister of Israel, David Ben Gurion, called attention to the fact that the tradition of the Law is no longer the unquestioned basis of modern Judaism. Both in Israel and in the Dispersion the orthodox, Law-abiding Jews are in a minority and can no longer set the standard of the nation. Christians will be wise, however, not to

welcome this over hastily. At first sight it may seem to make our task easier, and the modern secularized Jew may be more congenial and more approachable than the strictly observant Jew with his Talmudic training. Nevertheless, it would ill become us to despise the Law which is ' our schoolmaster to bring us unto Christ ', and to ignore what we have in common with those who are striving to build upon the foundation of the commandments. In spite of the difficulties, we must try to restate the Christian message in terms which will take account of the breakdown of Law, not only in Judaism but in Christianity as well.

It is not enough to say that the Law is obsolete. Obviously, religion and society are perishing for lack of something which was once provided, not in Judaism alone, by the Law with its religious sanction. Jews and Christians too are asking, What can take its place ? The question which perplexes the Jews is this : How can the Law be realized in the modern situation ? The answer of the Jewish authorities has so far failed to satisfy either those who wish to maintain the traditions intact or those who see the need for change.

It is only possible to suggest the outline of an answer. But it does seem as though Christianity can give guidance here, for it is a problem which the apostolic Church was called upon to face. In the New Testament we find St Paul confronted with the breakdown of the Law, and striving to check the resulting anarchy and licentiousness, by putting in the place of the Law the new righteousness which is by faith in Jesus Christ (e.g., I Cor. vi : 8–20 ; Romans vi–viii).

The Christian attitude to the Law is determined by Christ's claim to fulfil the Law. In the Pauline interpretation this involves two things :

(i) That the purpose of the Law for Israel is realized in Christ.

(ii) That thus the Law, having served its purpose, comes to an end and is merged in the new Christian order.

The Christian message to Israel, if it is to meet the need of today, must work out in detail the practical implications of this view. What is permanent, and what is merely transitory in the revelation of the Old Testament ? In what sense and to what extent is the Law eternally valid ? How is it related to the Covenant and the Promise, which Paul is careful to make independent of the Law (Gal. iii : 17) and unchangeable ? What about the laws attached to the Covenant, the Ten Commandments, the moral and humanitarian laws ? On what grounds do we differentiate them from the ceremonial and sacrificial and ritual laws ? And in what sense do we maintain that certain ordinances and institutions are taken up into the Christian scheme and transfigured, e.g., circumcision which becomes baptism, the passover which becomes the Lord's Supper, Israel itself which becomes the Church ?

Finally, in what sense is the Law abolished by Christ ? There is no doubt that the burden of the Law weighs heavily on conscientious Jews today, and many are going through a struggle very like that which St Paul describes (cf. Victor Gollancz's autobiography, *My Dear Timothy*). Many are haphazardly eclectic in their observance, and many more are observing traditions which have utterly lost any inner meaning. Christian freedom is one of the greatest gifts we have to offer them.

In reading the wistful writings of some Jewish thinkers, one is led to ask the question, Are they looking for a Gospel ? They know in their hearts that the Law is not the last word of God to them. There is a living revelation which was before the Law and which will be after it. Can we direct them to this living Word ?

2. The heart of the traditional Christian message to Israel deals with the question of the Messiah and Jesus Christ. The Jews are still a messianic people. ' It is the messianic hope which makes a Jew a Jew ', says Rabbi Maybaum. The expectation of the Messiah plays but a small part in their religion today. But the messianic hope has assumed other forms. It has been secularized in Zionism, it has been socialized in the kibbutzim, and it has been humanized and sentimentalized in the many pictures of the Messiah which are appearing in Jewish fiction. There

is still a small party in Israel which waits for the Messiah to rebuild the Temple. But the majority are content that it should remain in ruins, while they themselves, the people of the new Exodus, build a modern democracy in the Holy Land.

Nevertheless, there is no denying the interest in the figure of Jesus of Nazareth. The Jews today live in a land which is full of memories, and the memories of Jesus are inescapable. Not only in Israel, but throughout the world, the Jewish attitude to Jesus has changed :

(a) They have discovered that He is truly Jewish. This has been the most important result of recent scholarship so far as the Jews are concerned. His own people have claimed Him, and Israel is now face to face with a Christ who is no foreign invention, but a man of the people.

(b) They have gone so far as to admit in guarded terms that Jesus is beyond the normal categories, that He is the bearer of a revelation. While this cannot yet be said without fear of contradiction, there seems no doubt that Jewish thinkers are prepared to respect Jesus and to listen to His teaching, provided they can do so without disloyalty to Israel.

(c) They do not admit, however, that the Christian message is addressed to Israel. The most advanced position, as represented, e.g., by Joseph Klausner, recognizes Him as a revealer for the Gentiles, but allows Him no mission among His own people (cf. also Ignaz Maybaum, *The Jewish Mission*). Our reply must surely be that Jesus came primarily to the Jews, that His ministry was confined to the boundaries of Israel, with only rare exceptions, and that nothing in the Gospel records would justify the view that His purpose by-passed the Jews.

It has been suggested that the doctrine of the Second Coming corresponds closely to the messianic hope of the Jews, and there is much to be said in favour of a restatement of this doctrine in Jewish terms. The fact is that Christianity has divided the Advent into two parts, the coming in humility, which is already fulfilled, and the coming in glory which we still await. Judaism associates the Messiah exclusively with the coming in glory, and its rejection of Jesus is largely due to His failure to meet the conditions of the expectation. In spite of the fading of the messianic hope, the attitude of the Jews to the Church is still influenced by this criticism, which is applied to the failures of the Church :

> Where is Thy reign of peace
> And purity and love ?
> When shall all hatred cease,
> As in the realms above ?

3. The final section of the traditional Christian message deals with the hope of the Kingdom of God. Judaism avoids speculation about the last things, and as yet it is little influenced by the revival of interest in eschatology. Judaism is a faith for living, and even the expectation of the Kingdom is something to live by rather than something to die for.

Rightly or wrongly, the Jews criticize the Church for its otherworldliness, which seems to them to lead to acceptance of evil and an ignoble detachment in the struggle for righteousness. This criticism perhaps applies rather to Roman Catholicism than to Protestantism, but the truth in it must be taken to heart.

Hans Kosmala has pointed out (*The Jew in the Christian World*, p. 84) that the ' earthly mindedness ' of the Jew is often misinterpreted as materialism.

> In its origin it is nothing else than an expression of his instinctive love of life and his deeply-rooted appreciation of its gifts. In this the Jew excels all other races in the world. He feels entitled to enjoy the days of his life, even though their strength be no more than labour and sorrow. Through generations the Jew met death and persecution, but this has only intensified his desire and feeling for life ; although it seems a miracle of human history, it also explains how a people persecuted like the Jews should survive many of the persecuting nations.

The message to Israel must take full account of the feeling for the meaning and decisiveness of this present life which is so strong a feature in the Gospels. But it must also develop the suggestions which are found in Rom. xi and elsewhere on the place of Israel in the Kingdom of God; for there is much in the prophetic promises which political Zionism cannot satisfy, and Christ will yet be revealed as the Hope of Israel.

# APPENDIX I

## THE FIRST ASSEMBLY OF THE WORLD COUNCIL OF CHURCHES (AMSTERDAM, 1948)

### REPORT ON THE CHRISTIAN APPROACH TO THE JEWS

*Received by the Assembly and commended to the Churches for their serious consideration and appropriate action.*

### INTRODUCTION

A CONCERN for the Christian approach to the Jewish people confronts us inescapably, as we meet together to look with open and penitent eyes on man's disorder and to rediscover together God's eternal purpose for His Church. This concern is ours because it is first a concern of God made known to us in Christ. No people in His one world have suffered more bitterly from the disorder of man than the Jewish people. We cannot forget that we meet in a land from which 110,000 Jews were taken to be murdered. Nor can we forget that we meet only five years after the extermination of six million Jews. To the Jews our God has bound us in a special solidarity linking our destinies together in His design. We call upon all our churches to make this concern their own as we share with them the results of our too brief wrestling with it.

### 1. The Church's Commission to preach the Gospel to all men.

All of our churches stand under the commission of our common Lord, ' Go ye into all the world and preach the Gospel to every creature '. The fulfilment of this commission requires that we include the Jewish people in our evangelistic task.

### 2. The Special Meaning of the Jewish People for Christian Faith.

In the design of God, Israel has a unique position. It was Israel with whom God made His Covenant by the call of Abraham. It was Israel to whom God revealed His name and gave His Law. It was to Israel that He sent His Prophets with their message of judgment and of grace. It was Israel to whom He

13*                                    201

promised the coming of His Messiah. By the history of Israel God prepared the manger in which in the fullness of time He put the Redeemer of all mankind, Jesus Christ. The Church has received this spiritual heritage from Israel and is therefore in honour bound to render it back in the light of the Cross. We have, therefore, in humble conviction to proclaim to the Jews, 'The Messiah for whom you wait has come'. The promise has been fulfilled by the coming of Jesus Christ.

For many the continued existence of a Jewish people which does not acknowledge Christ is a divine mystery which finds its only sufficient explanation in the purpose of God's unchanging faithfulness and mercy (Romans ii : 25–29).

### 3. Barriers to be Overcome.

Before our churches can hope to fulfil the commission laid upon us by our Lord there are high barriers to be overcome. We speak here particularly of the barriers which we have too often helped to build and which we alone can remove.

We must acknowledge in all humility that too often we have failed to manifest Christian love towards our Jewish neighbours, or even a resolute will for common social justice. We have failed to fight with all our strength the age-old disorder of man which antisemitism represents. The churches in the past have helped to foster an image of the Jews as the sole enemies of Christ, which has contributed to antisemitism in the secular world. In many lands virulent antisemitism still threatens and in other lands the Jews are subjected to many indignities.

We call upon all the churches we represent to denounce antisemitism, no matter what its origin, as absolutely irreconcilable with the profession and practice of the Christian faith. Antisemitism is sin against God and man.

Only as we give convincing evidence to our Jewish neighbours that we seek for them the common rights and dignities which God wills for His children, can we come to such a meeting with them as would make it possible to share with them the best which God has given us in Christ.

### 4. The Christian Witness to the Jewish People.

In spite of the universality of our Lord's commission and of the fact that the first mission of the Church was to the Jewish people, our churches have with rare exceptions failed to maintain that mission. This responsibility should not be left largely to independent agencies. The carrying on of this mission by

special agencies has often meant the singling out of the Jews
for special missionary attention, even in situations where they
might well have been included in the normal ministry of the
Church.   It has also meant in many cases that the converts are
forced into segregated spiritual fellowship rather than being
included and welcomed in the regular membership of the
Church.

Owing to this failure our churches must consider the responsibility for missions to the Jews as a normal part of parish work,
especially in those countries where Jews are members of the
general community.   Where there is no indigenous church or
where the indigenous church is insufficient for this task it may
be necessary to arrange for a special missionary ministry from
abroad.

Because of the unique inheritance of the Jewish people the
churches should make provisions for the education of ministers
specially fitted for this task.   Provision should also be made for
Christian literature to interpret the Gospel to Jewish people.

Equally, it should be made clear to Church members that the
strongest argument in winning others for Christ is the radiance
and contagion of victorious living and the outgoing of God's
love expressed in personal human contacts.   As this is expressed
and experienced in a genuine Christian fellowship and community the impact of the Gospel will be felt.   For such a fellowship there will be no difference between a converted Jew and
other Church members, all belonging to the same Church and
fellowship through Jesus Christ.   But the converted Jew calls
for particular tenderness and full acceptance just because his
coming into the Church carries with it often a deeply wounding
break with family and friends.

In reconstruction and relief activities the churches must not
lose sight of the plight of Christians of Jewish origin, in view of
their special suffering.   Such provision must be made for their
aid as will help them to know that they are not forgotten in the
Christian fellowship.

## 5. *The Emergence of Israel as a State.*

The establishment of the State ' Israel ' adds a political
dimension to the Christian approach to the Jews and threatens
to complicate antisemitism with political fears and enmities.

On the political aspects of the Palestine problem and the
complex conflict of ' rights ' involved we do not undertake to
express a judgment.   Nevertheless we appeal to the nations to
deal with the problem not as one of expediency—political,

strategic, or economic—but as a moral and spiritual question that touches a nerve centre of the world's religious life.

Whatever position may be taken towards the establishment of a Jewish State and towards the ' rights ' and ' wrongs ' of Jews and Arabs, of Hebrew Christians and Arab Christians involved, the churches are in duty bound to pray and work for an order in Palestine as just as may be in the midst of our human disorder ; to provide within their power for the relief of the victims of this warfare without discrimination, and to seek to influence the nations to provide a refuge for ' Displaced Persons ' far more generously than has yet been done.

## RECOMMENDATIONS

We conclude this report with the recommendations which arise out of our first exploratory consideration of this ' concern ' of the churches.

*1. To the Member Churches of the World Council We Recommend :*

That they seek to recover the universality of our Lord's commission by including the Jewish people in their evangelistic work ;

That they encourage their people to seek for brotherly contact with and understanding of their Jewish neighbours, and co-operation in agencies combating misunderstanding and prejudice ;

That in mission work among the Jews they scrupulously avoid all unworthy pressures or inducements ;

That they give thought to the preparation of ministers well fitted to interpret the Gospel to Jewish people and to the provision of literature which will aid in such a ministry.

*2. To the World Council of Churches We Recommend :*

That it should give careful thought as to how it can best stimulate and assist the member churches in the carrying out of this aspect of their mission ;

That it give careful consideration to the suggestion made by the International Missionary Council that the World Council of Churches share with it a joint responsibility for the Christian approach to the Jews ;

That it be RESOLVED

that, in receiving the report of this Committee, the Assembly recognize the need for more detailed study by the World Council of Churches of the many complex problems which exist in the field of relations between Christians and Jews, and in particular of the following :

(*a*) the historical and present factors which have contributed to the growth and persistence of antisemitism, and the most effective means of combating this evil ;

(*b*) the need and opportunity in this present historical situation for the development of co-operation between Christians and Jews in civic and social affairs ;

(*c*) the many and varied problems created by establishment of a State of Israel in Palestine.

The Assembly therefore asks that these and related questions be referred to the Central Committee for further examination.

# APPENDIX II

## The Jewish Population

The figures given, though according to the Jewish Year Book, 1952, to statistics made by the Institute of Jewish Affairs, 1952, and to local information, can only be regarded as approximate. Few countries have a religious census, and it is also difficult to decide where to draw the line in reckoning those Jews who have no connection with the Synagogue. Another difficulty at present is that some countries have no Jewish organization owing to political circumstances.

| | |
|---|---:|
| WORLD JEWRY . . . . . | 11,600,000 |
| (Distributed in 97 different countries. This is about 6,400,000 fewer than before the war.) | |
| AMERICAS . . . . . . | 5,900,000 |
| United States of America . . . | 5,000,000 |
| Canada . . . . . | 205,000 |
| S. America . . . . | 650,000 |
| (Argentine 420,000 ; Brazil 110,000) | |
| AFRICA . . . . . . | 950,000 |
| Algeria . . . . . | 130,000 |
| French Morocco . . . . | 260,000 |
| Tunis . . . . . | 100,000 |
| Ethiopia . . . . . | 20,000 |
| South Africa . . . . | 105,000 |
| ASIA . . . . . . | 2,000,000 |
| Israel . . . . . | 1,450,000 |
| Persia . . . . . | 100,000 |
| AUSTRALIA (and NEW ZEALAND) . . | 56,000 |
| EUROPE . . . . . | 2,700,000 |
| Soviet Russia . . . . | 1,400,000 |
| Poland (formerly 3,000,000) . . | 35,000 |
| Rumania . . . . . | 190,000 |
| Hungary . . . . . | 100,000 |
| Czechoslovakia . . . . | 18,000 |
| Bulgaria . . . . . | 4,000 |
| Yugoslavia . . . . | 8,000 |
| Great Britain . . . . | 450,000 |
| France . . . . . | 240,000 |

EUROPE—*continued*

| | |
|---|---:|
| Belgium . . . . . . | 35,000 |
| Italy . . . . . . | 32,000 |
| European Turkey . . . . | 30,000 |
| Holland . . . . . . | 25,000 |
| Switzerland . . . . . | 22,000 |
| Germany (formerly 600,000) . . | 20,000 |
| Sweden . . . . . . | 15,000 |
| Austria . . . . . . | 12,000 |
| Greece . . . . . . | 8,000 |
| Denmark . . . . . . | 5,000 |
| Norway . . . . . . | 1,000 |
| Others (Portugal, Spain, Finland, Luxembourg, Eire, Rhodes) . . . | 50,000 |

Of the European Jews only about 950,000 are living in Western Europe, half of which number are in Great Britain and 240,000 in France.

# INTERNATIONAL MISSIONARY COUNCIL

## COMMITTEE ON THE CHRISTIAN APPROACH TO THE JEWS
### 1954

#### OFFICERS

*Hon. Chairman :* Dr CONRAD HOFFMANN, New York
*Chairman :* Rev. R. CLEPHANE MACANNA, Edinburgh
*Vice-Chairmen :* Rev. C. T. LEBER, New York ; Rev. BIRGER PERNOW, Stockholm
*Director :* Rev. GÖTE HEDENQUIST, Uppsala, Sweden
*Editor of ' News Sheet' :* Rev. ROBERT SMITH, Edinburgh

The Committee consists of the following three Sections :

#### EUROPEAN SECTION

| | |
|---|---|
| Rev. R. Bakker, Holland | Rev. R. Rasmussen, Denmark |
| Rev. R. Brunner, Switzerland | Prof. K. H. Rengstorf, Germany |
| Rev. J. Delpech, France | Rev. N. Rosef, Norway |

Rev. J. H. Grolle, Holland

#### BRITISH SECTION

| | |
|---|---|
| Rev. Canon J. McLeod Campbell, D.D. | Mr H. Newmark |
| Rev. W. A. Curtis | Rev. W. R. Newton |
| Rev. H. L. Ellison | Rev. Stanley A. Smith |

Mr L. B. Greaves

#### AMERICAN SECTION

| | |
|---|---|
| Rev. Nils E. Bergstrom | Dr Claude H. Pritchard |
| Rev. Luther A. Gotwald | Mrs Arthur M. Sherman |
| Prof. Walter M. Horton | Dr E. Graham Wilson |

Mr Paul O. Madsen

*Representatives of the World Council of Churches*
*Europe :* Dr Adolf Freudenberg
*Great Britain :* The Very Rev. Dean C. Witton-Davies
*America :* Rev. Charles W. Arbuthnot

*The International Hebrew Christian Alliance*
*Europe :* Rev. H. D. Leuner
*Great Britain :* Rev. Harcourt Samuel
*America :* Rev. Jacob Peltz

*Members at large :* Rev. G. A. F. Knight, New Zealand ; Rev. Hans Kosmala, Jerusalem
*Office Secretaries :* Dr J. W. Decker, 156 Fifth Avenue, *New York* 10
Miss P. Shepherd, Edinburgh House, 2 Eaton Gate, London S.W.1
*Director's office :* Idrottsgatan 33D, *Uppsala*, Sweden

# INDEX

ABRAHAM, 13, 14, 21, 28, 29, 30, 32, 38, 41, 42, 44, 69, 141, 193, 201
Abrahams, I., 52, 119
Akiba, Rabbi, 40, 51
Algiers, 173
American Committee on the Ch. Appr. to the Jews, 175
Conf. of Christians and Jews, 131
Reform Rabbis, 50
Amitié Judéo Chrétienne, 136
Amsterdam, 1948, 5, 119, 134, 137, 168, 172, 193, 201-5
Anglican Church, 138, 139, 175
Anti-Judaism, 41, 154, 155-8
antisemitism, 18, 36, 41, 68, 77, 78, 103, 119-21, 130, 131, 133, 134, 148, 149, 151, 154, 157-8, 160, 168, 170, 177, 184, 185, 186, 192, 193, 202, 203, 205
Arab-Israel War, 79, 80, 91, 204
Arab refugee problem, 120, 204
Asch, S., 101
assimilation, 36, 54, 69, 77, 144-9, 154, 157-61, 181
Atlantic City Conf., 1931, 137
Australia, 132, 173, 206
Austria, 148, 169, 170, 171, 173, 207

BAR KOCHBA, 42, 65
Barth, Karl, 62, 193
Basle, 1947, 159
Belgium, 172, 207
Ben Azzai, 51, 76
Gurion, 92, 93, 94, 195
Zvi, 138
Ben-Chorin, Schalom, 49, 52-3, 54, 58, 59, 60
Bene-Brak, 64
Berdyaev, 193
Bergman, H., 48, 51, 52, 57-8, 62
Berlin synod, 1950, 170
Billerbeck, 119
Bistritzki, N., 100
Box, Canon, 153
British Council of Christians and Jews, 123-5, 130-1, 133, 137, 182
of Churches, 137, 139
Jews Society, 173
Mandate, 78, 79, 88
Brod, M., 100
brotherhood, 55, 59, 91, 117-8, 128, 129, 136, 140, 157
Buber, Martin, 53, 54, 61, 69, 72, 100, 117-18, 142
Budapest-Warsaw Conferences, 137

CANADA, 146, 206
Women's Inter-Ch. C'cil, 175
Caro, Joseph, 65, 66

Christian literature, 60, 99, 203
missionary work, 85, 87, 108-9, 137, 162, 164, 169, 174, 189, 190, 202
youth organizations, 130, 186
*Christian News from Israel*, 138
*Christian Year Book, A*, 189
Church
and Synagogue, 141, 144, 152
local, 157-8, 160, 162-3, 166, 168, 171-2, 179-88
of England, 130, 153, 172, 173
of Scotland, 130, 172, 173
Church(es), indigenous, 155, 164, 165, 173, 203
Cohen, H., 49
Cohen, I., 143
Cohon, S. S., 50, 51, 56
*Columbus Platform*, 50, 54, 59
Commission on Religious Freedom, 133
Committee on Work among the Jews, 172
*Common Ground*, 131
*Common Sense*, 131-2
community of faith, 106, 108
Conference of Miss. Soc. in Gt. Britain and Ireland, 155, 172
Congregational Church, U.S.A., 175
conversion(s), 23, 44, 52, 53, 109, 144-56, 161-5, 187-8, 203
co-operation, inter-religious, 20, 21, 128-9
Councils of Christians and Jews, 127, 132-3, 136, 182
of Social Service, 138
Creizenach, M., 66
Czechoslovakia, 171, 206

DALMAN, Prof., 144
Danby, H., 119
Day of Atonement, 64
de la Roi, J. F. A., 144
Declaration of Human Rights, 23, 125
Delitzsch, Franz, 152
Diaspora, 38, 81, 82, 84, 88
dispersion, 36, 38, 51, 57, 77, 80, 82, 190, 195
dogma of Judaism, 49-52, 72

EBIONISM, 154
ecumenical movement, 164, 189, 190
Einsbruch, 186
Eisenstein, Ira, 56
election of Israel, 28, 29, 30, 31, 33, 35, 38, 40, 43, 51, 67, 68, 71, 159, 192-3
emancipation, 65, 66, 107, 149
*emuna*, 53
eschatology, 15, 58, 59, 60, 61, 192, 194, 199